MISS RONA

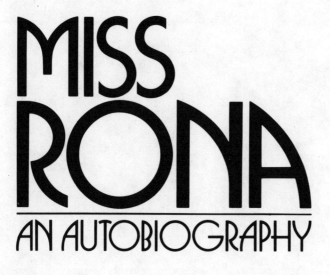

MISS RONA

AN AUTOBIOGRAPHY

BY
RONA BARRETT

NASH PUBLISHING, LOS ANGELES

Library of Congress Catalog Card Number: 73-93029
International Standard Book Number: 0-8402-1336-0

Published simultaneously in the United States and Canada
by Nash Publishing Corporation, 9255 Sunset Boulevard
Los Angeles, California 90069

Printed in the United States of America

First Printing

To my sister Marcia, whom I have written little about, but adore . . .

To my Uncle Joe, who believed when all others didn't . . .

To my friends—they know who they are—who believed, likewise . . .

And above all to the good Lord, who always gave me His strength, though I did not recognize it all the time.

PROLOGUE

"An *inch,* Rona. Please, just let me put it in one inch!"

The man pleading with me was one of Hollywood's top male sex symbols for over twenty years and still is, as well as being a great actor.

I'd been staying with him and his wife at their lush Acapulco suite. Their bedroom and mine adjoined the same terrace. I had walked to the balcony at about 3:00 A.M., sure that they'd be asleep.

I was undergoing a life-and-death crisis that night. For eight years—*eight years*—I had been going almost exclusively with a man who was split down the middle of his psyche with a Madonna-whore complex that would have boggled Sigmund Freud. While he publicly put the make on dozens upon dozens of female stars and starlets, he kept our relationship strictly private—even clandestine. Though he was by no stretch of the imagination Italian, he treated me like many Mafia men treat their wives. I was to be the good girl he could depend on for aid, and it seemed as if he always left after I gave his confidence an adrenalin boost. Marriage was something for the future. Future? All I could think of was how many years had slipped into the past.

I could not stay in bed, couldn't lie still. Even to be with him and *not* be touched—watch him touch himself, as he often did, watch him tease me as I'm sure few women have ever been teased—was better than *alone*. I had become addicted to his perversions. But, as always, when I most needed him he wasn't there. I was desperate. The feelings I'd sublimated and suppressed for fifteen years as I rose to Hollywood's pinnacle were taking me over totally.

And now, standing so close that I could actually feel his intense breathing and clad only in a too-open bathrobe, was a *bona fide* man, a brain *and* a body *and,* most of all, a dynamic personality which welded them together dazzlingly. He was a *real* hero, a modern day gladiator and gunslinger all rolled up into one. At the very peak of his power and prowess. And just ten seconds before, he had said to me, "I've got to have *you,* Rona." *Me,* the crippled, plain, fat kid from Queens, who—from Eddie Fisher to one of Lyndon B. Johnson's top cohorts to the man I'd been involved with now for three thousand days—had never sexually or emotionally experienced a male secure enough in his maleness to make me feel like a *female.*

I answered in a shocked whisper: "Your wife's sleeping not ten feet away."

"We'll go to *your* room," he shot back.

"We're *friends.*"

"I've got to have it, Rona. I feel like I'll die if I don't! If you won't let me screw you, then just let me put it in an inch. Please. Just one inch."

"No. Absolutely *no.*"

Melodramatic?

Gentle reader, let me tell it to you *exactly* like it is before I go one word further: If you *are* gentle, if your psyche is marked HANDLE WITH CARE, then close this book and never open it again. Even leave the room if someone begins to talk about it. Because underneath, and not far underneath, I'm *too* gentle. I need tenderness and understanding as much as any woman, maybe more. But I'm writing this sometimes gross, sometimes shocking book to preserve precisely that part of me. It's ironic, but until you can free those final monsters within the jungle of yourself, your life, your soul is up for grabs.

There's a term in acting: *Risking yourself.* I can count on the fingers of my two hands, and still have some left over, the number of actors or actresses I've met who have ever risked in front of a camera, let alone in front of the bathroom mirror. I thought I risked at the age of eight when two prominent doctors told my mother they didn't think I'd live past nine and I screamed back at them, "Important people don't die at nine! I'm going to live . . . do you hear me? . . . *Hear?*"

I risked when at thirty-five I went to a psychiatrist, something I had vowed I'd never do—because I finally had to admit to myself that I was an emotional cripple, that I'd been crawling for men all my life.

Yet those risks were easy compared to this book. Fighting my way to Hollywood's peak was easy compared to this. In a way, I had risen *above* the glittering stars because I encompassed them, understood them, yet remained apart, untouchable. Was that why they wanted me? It took twenty years, working seven days a week, seventeen hours a day, to reach *that* pinnacle. Yet at the end, I hadn't encompassed, hadn't understood myself. I was split. Apart not only from them, but from Rona. Not just untouchable. *Untouched.*

This book is my risk.

This book, about the *real* pinnacle, the one I hope to reach, began when I faced myself, let myself be truly touched. For years, after the TV show was taped, the magazines published, the celebrities interviewed and entertained and on their way, I would throw myself on the kingsize bed of my Beverly Hills home and weep like the helpless little girl I still was. I didn't know it then, but that was *easy*. To bear pain. It nearly killed me, but it was *easy* compared to the risk of finding—and losing—happiness! I chose to find happiness, to be open completely, like an animal gutted to its center, the organs showing but still pulsing and alive, waiting, desperately waiting to be sewn up, yet knowing that somehow it has to sew itself.

With this book, I take needle and thread in my hands.

I have known unsurpassable exaltation in my life.

I have known unbearable pain.

If you think *you* can take it, Risking Reader, then crawl, stumble, walk, and then run with me through the jungles of my inside. And maybe your own. When we arrive at the clearing, I promise you'll know that *nothing* is gross, except our own refusal to face ourselves.

As there wasn't anything gross about "Please. Just one inch!" I may not have known myself then, but I understood him. We're even closer now than before. He was one of the few to help me—no strings attached—when I first came to Hollywood, because he felt I not only told it like it was, but told it that way because I believed in what Hollywood once was, believed in heroes and heroines, in people like *him,* in life being as dramatic as possible. *Melodramatic.* He so much wanted that kind of Hollywood—that kind of world. For above and beyond all my host's manly accomplishments and erudition and charisma, he was a beautiful little boy.

Yet, like a little boy, he wanted what he wanted when he wanted it! He's no different on the screen. Little boys can hurt others or themselves if they don't have grown-ups around. That night I had to be the grown-up. His wife, lying little more than the length of our bodies away, was my friend.

His friend, too. Even though he "had" to have me, Rona Barrett was far from this remarkable boy-man's first female obsession. On a dozen occasions he had thrown his incredible charms at the feet of some special female. And she'd always ended up at his feet. Happily.

Until his wife came upon the scene. His wife never threatened, never competed. She understood her superstar, superman husband too well. She has to be one of Hollywood's wisest women. For she made friends, *real* friends, with each and every mistress. And because she was genuine, she got into their heads even more than he did. Eventually, every single girl stepped aside, saying to him, "I just can't get into bed with you one more time. I can't do it to *her*." So this couple acquired one of the most tightly knit yet strangest circles of friends in Hollywood: All of his former mistresses and their present husbands or lovers!

Yes, my loins *were* stirred by his life-or-death proposition that life-or-death 3:00 A.M. But I had already been inextricably involved for eight years with a man who was willing to stick it in only an inch.

And it was killing me.

I was thirty-three years old.

I wanted to go all the way.

This book is *it* . . .

CHAPTER ONE

It was May of 1971.

There were a lot of people who were saying I had reached the top and that nothing could stop me from staying there either. It was only a matter of doing the same thing tomorrow and the day after tomorrow and maybe the month or even the year after tomorrow—preparing my national TV show, overseeing my magazines, talking to the people who would talk to me now before they talked to anyone else.

Winchell was dying of cancer. It had seemed more to have grown out of him than into him. For several years now he'd had assistance from his staff in writing his columns most of the time anyway, and, as the Hearst empire died, Walter's empire seemed to also.

Hedda Hopper was dead and Louella Parsons was living in a nursing home. She was dead in a different kind of way.

Dorothy Kilgallen had committed suicide, consciously or subconsciously.

Earl Wilson and Hy Gardner were powerful, but not *that* powerful and never would be because they wouldn't risk. They'd finally rather go to a restaurant or a reception, than go deep inside the human soul.

There were new Winchells and Wilsons on the horizon, of course. I had competitors. But they had to compete with me, not I with them. And, frankly, they weren't doing too well. Joyce Haber of the *Los Angeles Times* once said that the difference between my audience and hers was that mine didn't read. And she was right. They don't read her column, which often duplicates much of my material.

Maybe the license plate on my Rolls said it best: MS RONA.

As I write these words now, I can't say that the license plate and the Rolls or my home in Beverly Hills or the dignified Chinese couple who worked there or my *alte rich* neighbors or everything that went with all of it didn't mean a hell of a lot to me. Seeing my name on two magazines everytime I walked by a newsstand, my face on TV every night in just about every major city—to say nothing of my being one of the ten best-known Americans in one of those top TVQ type polls. Oh, yeah, it meant something to me. Then it meant almost *everything*.

Because put them all together, with a dash of tenure and a push of promotion and they added up to . . . the pinnacle. What more could I want than that?

Okay, so my personal life was usually crummy. So I came home and cried most evenings, instead of reaping the benefits of what went on from six in the morning until six at night.

But *I* was the only one who knew it. There were *some* good moments away from work. The important thing was that, except for a three-week AFTRA strike in 1967 where I absolutely *couldn't* work, I hadn't missed a single show in all the years I'd been on television.

I finally did the week of May 14, 1971. I think I attempted suicide. I say "I think" because to this day I'm not really sure what happened.

CHAPTER TWO

I stood in front of the mirror above my mother's dressing table. I didn't know how long I'd been standing there. It was the only mirror in the house in which I could see practically all of myself. Only the bottom half of my legs were missing.

Somehow I couldn't take my eyes off the reflection and I found myself saying, "Oh, God, am I really that ugly?"

The doctor had told my mother it was a new kind of lightweight brace. It only weighed nine and a half pounds, but on me it wouldn't make any difference if it had weighed twenty. I was just over four feet tall and nearly as wide. With the brace, I looked like Miss Four by Five. I tried not to cry. I didn't want my tears to fall on the new dress my mother had bought me. Besides, how could I go to school with red eyes? But the tears welled up anyway and slowly began to trickle down my cheeks. Everything seemed so grotesque: the hairline of my dark brown hair seemed to meet the bridge of my nose. And the small bump on my nose which seemed so large in profile stood out like a giant wart. And my cheeks. They were so fat and round—not even an apple was shaped like that.

"Oh, God. Will I always be ugly? Won't I ever be beautiful? Why, God? Why me?"

My mother, at that precise moment, walked into the bedroom.

"What are you staring at, Rona?" she asked.

"I look so terrible, Momma. I can't go to school today."

"How ridiculous, sweetheart. You don't look any different than before—maybe a little heavier, but your teacher already knows you'll be wearing this brace for the next six weeks. You have nothing to worry about."

"But, Momma. The kids. I know them. You don't. They'll make fun. They make fun when I try to walk up the stairs. Now they'll make worse fun. Please, Momma, don't make me go to school today."

"Rona, I told you you had nothing to worry about. C'mon, I'll even walk with you to school. You'll just take your time walking up the stairs and nothing will be any different."

My mother helped me on with my coat. Autumn had just gone and winter was almost upon us. I was only grateful that it hadn't yet started snowing. The coat, of course, didn't close. My mother had thought of buying me a larger dress to wear over the cumbersome brace, but she hadn't thought about outdoor apparel. Besides, the school was only a block away from our apartment and I had enough fat on me to keep me warm just getting back and forth.

"She really won't freeze to death," I could hear my mother saying to herself.

The cold wind whipped around my face and slammed into my chest. I was almost thankful I was wearing the ugly thing. At least it kept me from feeling the wind bite through my clothes and into my skin.

As we walked down the block I grabbed hold of my mother's hand, afraid to look up because if I'd miss my step and trip I wouldn't know how to get up. Clinging to her arm, I nervously asked her, "But what will happen when it snows again, Ma? What if there's a fire drill? What if there's an air raid drill? What am I going to do, Ma?"

"Listen, Rona. For the last six months you've been going to school, you've been managing very nicely. Like a big girl. You already know Mrs. Adenoff is aware of your condition and she's prepared to help you. I already got permission from the principal to allow you to go into the classroom ahead of schedule so you don't have to walk up the stairs when the rest of the other kids do. Now what more do you want from me? I'm telling you, there's nothing to be frightened of."

My mother left me off at the entrance to P.S. 5. It was perhaps the oldest primary school in the borough of Queens and God only knew if it wasn't the oldest school in existence in all of New York. It certainly looked it. Despite its insides being annually painted, the brick looked as old as the first White House.

I looked around at my mother. There was a big lump in her throat, I could tell, but she wouldn't permit herself to cry in front of me. It was bad enough she cried every night when she went to bed. Why had God done this to her? I could hear her cry. Little did she realize how many nights I could hear her from the next bedroom. Little did she know how many times I'd hear her cry to my dad, "Why, Harry? Why us? What did I do to deserve this? What's going to happen to her when she grows up, Harry? Do you think any man's going to want her? Do you think she'll be able to have children like other girls have? And if she does, will they be normal or will they be afflicted with whatever it is that she has? Oh, Harry. What are we going to do?"

I had a difficult time discerning my father's comments.

He spoke so low. His voice was so cultured while my mother's seemed so harsh and crude. I often wondered how my parents ever got together. But why God had chosen them for *me* was still the unsolved mystery I was determined to find an answer to.

"Good-bye, Ma. I'll see you later."

"Take care, sweetheart. And walk up the stairs slowly. You have plenty of time before the bell will ring."

"Yes, Ma. 'Bye."

I looked at the stairs before me. They were the thing I most despised in my life. The thought of climbing any stairs gripped my stomach in a fierce ache; my legs would suddenly feel heavier than they were and my temples would begin to pound. *Hurry up! Get up those stairs,* my brain would command. And the more my brain tried to tell me to hurry up, the slower I seemed to move. It seemed like an eternity, if only I knew what eternity really was. Every day I'd try to make it a game, counting each step. And the closer I got toward the top, the more relieved I would become, but the pounding would get heavier and heavier until I was at last on the top landing. There were thirty-two steps in all, but there might as well have been a million and thirty-two.

At five, I hadn't quite learned how to control my muscles to get them to look as if they worked normally. I could get up a flight of stairs by practically crawling up on all fours like an animal, or I could drag one foot at a time onto each step, using my little arms to pull all my weight along the bannister. Having the other kids see me climb this way made me want to die, so I had made a bargain with my mother. If they wanted me to go to public school, they would have to elicit permission for

me to get to my classroom before everyone else and leave
either before the bell rang or way after the other kids
had left the school.

It was extremely difficult for my parents to explain to
Principal Burns what was wrong with their only child.
If the hundreds of doctors they had seen didn't know,
how could they put a name to their child's affliction? All
anyone knew was that I had a muscular deficiency, and
it looked like it was getting worse as I grew older instead
of better.

According to my parents, they had noticed something
wrong with me when I was about nine months old. I
seemed to drag one leg as I tried to lift myself up in my
crib. My mother at first paid little attention. She thought
it might be her imagination. But as I got older, she noticed
that if someone even blew on me I would fall. And where
I fell that's where I'd stay. Totally incapable of pulling
myself up, I would just lie there like a deadweight. That's
when my mother decided she'd better take me to a special-
ist and have him check me out. The first doctor thought
my mother was crazy.

"There's nothing wrong with your daughter," he told
her. "She's as normal as anyone else. I think she's just
too fat. You're feeding her too much."

But my mother knew he was wrong. My abnormal
symptoms became more prevalent, yet there was not a
doctor who could diagnose the problem.

A new orthopedic surgeon she found said that I was
suffering from a curvature of the spine and if I wore a
brace it was more than likely that everything would eventually be normal. While my mother didn't believe a word
the doctor said, she was willing to listen to him—to anything! And everybody! She let the doctor order the brace

for me. In her mind, she'd already tried everything else within her power. Maybe I did have a curved spine.

Then in December, as the first term of kindergarten closed, another doctor came up with another brilliant suggestion. "Let's operate on the child," he said. "We'll know once and for all what's wrong with her then."

He was a young surgeon and had been highly recommended to my parents by our family doctor. He worked out of Children's Hospital in Manhattan, where a lot of fancy research was being conducted on unknown diseases. The doctor had told my mother exactly what he would do.

"Believe me, Mrs. Burstein, you have nothing to worry about. Rona will be in the hospital for only three weeks. It's a simple operation. All I'll do is make an incision on her leg and remove a piece of tissue and a piece of muscle and we'll examine them in our laboratory and I know we'll have an answer for you then. The child's biggest problem seems to be in her legs, and that's why I'd like to take a biopsy from her thigh. That's all that's involved. Really, it's very simple. I suggest you and your husband think about it and let me know. It's the only way to determine what the problem really is."

My mother and father talked it over at dinner that night. They finally decided to ask me what I wanted.

My first reaction was "Wonderful! Wonderful! I've never been in a hospital before. It'll be fun. I can play with doctors and nurses and there'll be other kids. Oh, yes, Mommy. Let's do it. What do we have to lose? Yes, Mommy. Let me be operated on."

So my mother asked the principal for permission to take me out of school for three weeks. It was almost Christmastime so I wouldn't have to miss too much. Miss Burns said, "Of course."

The operation proved nothing. The doctors didn't know any more afterwards than they had before. And the scar on my leg was so ugly I wondered how I would ever be able to wear a bathing suit again. They had cut my leg open right at the top of my thigh, and the day I was released an intern forgot to tell my mother to bring me back a week later to have the stitches taken out. It was almost a month later that the young surgeon saw me for a final checkup, and when he discovered the stitches were still in he was in a state of shock. He took my mother out of the cubbyhole where he'd been examining me, but I could hear him anyway.

"I'm really sorry about this, Mrs. Burstein. I didn't know the stitches hadn't been removed. They're the kind that leave bad marks. I hope they won't be too bad, but the scar will probably be much bigger than it should have been."

"What in the world did my husband and I pay you for, Doctor? Not only did you cut up my baby, but she'll be scarred for life, you bastard!" My mother never cursed.

"Now listen, Mrs. Burstein, I told you I'm sorry!"

"Sorry. What do you know what it's like to be sorry? Do you have a cripple for a kid?"

The scar on my leg was nothing compared to the scar that was forming in my head.

Mrs. Adenoff was already seated behind her desk when I finally arrived at the classroom with my new brace. But before I could say much to Mrs. Adenoff, the school bell rang, and by the time I got my coat off and hung up in the closet, the classroom was filling up.

Mrs. Adenoff took attendance first. The class was arranged in alphabetical order, and I sat at the first table with three other kids whose names began with A and B.

I had been thinking to myself, as I tried to slouch in the little wooden chair, that maybe no one had noticed I looked different. Then to my horror I heard Mrs. Adenoff say, "Now, children, I don't want you to ask Rona any questions. Rona looks a little different today because she's wearing a brace, and so she won't be able to play games with us. Stand up, Rona."

Slowly, I lifted myself out of my chair and walked towards Mrs. Adenoff's desk. And then the laughing began, nervous giggles at first, becoming louder, until from the back of the room one of the boys yelled, in sing-song fashion, "Rona's a fatty! Rona's a cripple! Rona's wearing a girdle!"

Then the whole class burst into laughter, and the tears which had been welling in my eyes could find no dam to hold them back. Like a swollen rushing river, they poured down my cheeks.

"Children! Children! Stop it! Stop it!" Mrs. Adenoff yelled, pounding her fist on the desk. But the laughing did not stop. I just stood there, frozen, when suddenly I felt Mrs. Adenoff's arms swing around me. I wanted to push her away—pity was not my game, not what I was looking for—but somehow I couldn't move. Then, just as swiftly as my tears had started, they dried up and I wrenched myself free and walked back to my chair and sat down, silently praying the noon bell would ring soon.

At 12:05, when I was sure I wouldn't have to face anyone, I put on my coat. I walked out the door and down the thirty-two steps. *If only all stairs went down instead of up. If only all stairs were escalators I'd never have anything to worry about again in my life.*

Outside, the winds seemed to have gotten stronger. I tried pulling my coat around me as tight as it would go.

But it still wouldn't button. So I pulled my collar up around my neck and proceeded to cross the street and walk the one block home. Now if only I didn't fall. The winds were pushing at me and I could hardly keep my balance, when suddenly I noticed at least a dozen boys and girls from my class following me from across the street. My heart started to beat very fast and the more I tried to quicken my pace the longer it seemed to take me to walk the block. And then, they all crossed over and were walking behind me. One of the boys was leading the pack and he reminded me of a bad Pied Piper.

Dear God. Please let me get home without any trouble.

I was only two buildings away when the Pied Piper yelled, "Hey, fatty. We're gonna get ya. We wanna feel your titties. We wanna know if it's really a girdle you're wearing or you're just plain fat and lookin' for sympathy. Hey, fatty. We're gonna get ya."

"Just one more building," I murmured to myself. "God, let me get home. Please."

But God was busy someplace else. I didn't make it. Just as I hit the walkway to the building entrance, I found myself surrounded by them, each of them now equipped with long sticks. They began poking and taunting me, hitting and jabbing me, running away and then thrusting forward once more. I looked around for something to hold onto or for someone to help me. I couldn't scream for my mother; our apartment faced the rear of the building. And the doorman wasn't around. Why wasn't he around when I needed him? Why wasn't he around when anybody needed him?

There was a scrawny tree nearby and I aimed myself at it and grabbed on for dear life. But the kids formed a semicircle around me and kept poking me with their sticks as if I were some pincushion. I tried to lean away, and only then did I discover, with shock and mounting fury, that I was literally becoming glued to the freshly tarred tree!

Mr. Anderson, the building's superintendent, was a stickler for maintaining the pathetic, city-suffocated lawn and trees which lined the walkway. He was particularly obsessed with tree trunks, and he rushed to tar the damaged bark whenever and wherever he discovered a new set of initials had been carved.

Realizing I was stuck, the mob increased their taunting. Just then, Harriet Brookman, my closest girlfriend, walked by. Perceiving the situation, she darted at the crowd, screaming, "You dumb kids. How can you do that to her? You know she's not strong enough to fight back! Get away! Get away!" She pushed through, waving her hands wildly about. The semicircle broke and Harriet pulled me from the tree, dragging me toward the doorway. But by then, I had grown too weak. My legs finally gave way, and I fell to the flagstone walk.

Harriet tried desperately to lift me, but with the added weight of the brace I couldn't manage it. I appealed to one of the boys for help, but he only laughed and said I looked like a clown lying sprawled out like that. Unfortunately, the stronger Harriet tried to make herself, the heavier I became. It never failed when I was dependent on someone to help me get up. But somehow we succeeded, and it was only by the skin of our teeth or perhaps the reappearance of the Almighty, that we made it through the electronically controlled front door.

Inside at last, I felt somewhat safe, but I was so enraged I wanted to kill. Who? I did not know. Was it my mother, because she wasn't around to rescue me? Was it the kids, because of their stupidity? Or was it God, because He hadn't made me like everybody else?

Whatever it was, whoever it was, I cried bitterly. I slowly grabbed hold of the bannister and pulled myself up one step, then turning I screamed at the kids who continued to pound on the front door, jeering at me through the glass. "You really don't know who I am. But someday you will. Someday, so help me. I'll be so important . . . so famous . . . none of you will ever be able to touch me again!"

Through the door, I heard one of the boys yell back, "Ah, shut up, cripple. You're nobody and you never will be!"

I knew that it was no use arguing with a bunch of dummies. I turned away and dragged myself up the steps, one at a time, vowing with each one to the third floor that no matter what it took, someday I'd be SOMEONE! So help me God.

So help me, dear God! I'll be someone!

CHAPTER THREE

After that, everything seemed to take a turn for the better. . . .

If I were writing a Hollywood movie of the forties that line would come next. But as a grammar school kid in the forties, the sun didn't suddenly shine through simply because I had taken the first step against being panicked by the huge, dark cloud over my life. The clouds were still there, huger and darker than ever, as a matter of fact. So, when I was eight years old, my mother and father decided to take the boldest step possible to find out what was wrong with me.

For several years before that, our lives had been suspended in a kind of limbo. My parents had taken me to so many doctors and specialists that there didn't seem to be anything left to do.

"But we've *got* to do something, Harry," my mother would say to my father at night when they were alone in their room.

"Well, *what?*"

It was almost the very same conversation night after night. "There's *got* to be someone out there with an answer," my mother would go on. "Aren't you the one who studied economics and said for every problem there's an answer?"

My father would be silent.

"Your customers, Harry. Ask your customers if they know of some doctor." My father was in the grocery business just like his mother had been.

"I've asked them, Ida. Do you think she's just *your* child? Don't you think I want to know, too? Don't you think I want to see her climb stairs and run like other children?" Then, as always, they began arguing. It would get pretty heated. I had to admire my mother for never giving up, but at times her constant harassment of my father almost drove him crazy.

"I'll never rest until I see that girl normal, Harry."

"Fine! But am *I* ever going to get some rest? And what about *her?* Everyone in the building can hear you. It's enough Rona has to live with what she's got. But you keep reminding her, reminding her, reminding her!"

"Don't yell at me! You think it's a picnic carrying an eight-year-old kid in your arms when it's snowing yet, three flights of stairs to a train and *shlep* her to a hospital where a bunch of important-looking doctors don't know what the hell they're talking about while *you* are back in the store talking to the pretty women or playing the stock market!"

"Don't you talk about my stocks." My father was very sensitive about his playing the stock market. I think it had become a substitute for not being an economist or a C.P.A.

"I'll talk about anything I want," my mother shouted back. "Do you think I don't know where the extra money goes? We should be rich except you fart it away on your *fakakta* stocks!"

"That's a lie, Ida, and you know it. The money is going for that poor kid."

"Aw, what does it matter? All you know is to go to

your grocery store, come home at night to your supper on the table and sit and read the paper. I tell you we've got to do something for Rona, because *I'm* the one who has to dress her in the morning, watch her stumble up off the floor like a little wounded soldier, wait for her to come home with the other kids calling her *cripple.* But all you want is a little peace and quiet at night and your dinner!"

"Ida," my father said suddenly, raising his voice as he did so rarely. "I could cut your tongue out sometimes. I care as much about the kid as anybody in the world. But all you do is nag. I've asked *every*body. We've been *every*where. You tell me the answer. You tell me where there's somebody and I'll have her there tomorrow!"

"Do *I* have to come up with all the answers? It isn't enough what I've done already? *Shlepped* her everywhere, to every hospital in this city. You're the *man.* Oh yeah, you can blow big about *trends*—is that what you call them, big shot?—that explain why the country is going to be prosperous or why we had a depression and all that *cockarei.* But you don't know enough to find a doctor who can help one kid be normal like other kids."

"That's right, I don't, Ida, I *don't.* And all your vicious, fish market screaming doesn't change anything in the whole world!"

"Maybe I scream, big shot, but I'll tell you this: You better think about the future with Rona, not about all your trends in the stock market. Do you know what this girl's future is going to be like? Do you know she is going to be living here her whole life? An old maid, Harry, an *old maid.* It's bad enough that I have a sister who hasn't married yet and another one who married a bum. But to have a *daughter* who is an *old maid!* Do you hear me, Harry? Do you understand what I am saying? I—want—Rona—Burstein—to—be—healthy—like—other—kids—and—I—want—boys—should—like—her—and—I—want—her—to—get—married—some—day—and—have—a—kid—of—her—own."

I thought I heard what might have been tears from my father. "Ida . . . I know . . . I want it, too . . . I'll try to ask someone new in the morning . . . Maybe there's someone I haven't thought of. . . ."

And then, as happened once in a blue moon, my mother showed her soft side. "You're a good man, Harry," she said so softly I could hardly hear. I pressed my ear to the wall. "I know you love her as much as I do. But loving her isn't enough, don't you see? We have to make that love into strong legs for Rona and at least a decent-looking body. So help me, I don't know if she can ever have children. Probably she wasn't meant to. But we'll cross that bridge when we come to it. Right now we got to take all this pain and this love and make it into something for Rona. She's a *child,* Harry. She can't do it for herself. It's completely up to us. But now, come here, Harry."

And that's how it would go, night after night, month after month.

Until one night something new was added.

They had gone on and on as usual and in the end were more like cat and dog than ever. I actually wondered if they would physically strike each other, because my mother was pulling out all the stops and my father wasn't going to take it.

"Do you know what you are, Harry? You're not a success. You're a loser. You like everybody to think you're a big success because you make some money and have the biggest store in the neighborhood. If they think it, then you can think it. But you're no success. You wanted to be something else. That's why you throw all your money away in the stocks. And that's why you're going to let Rona be a loser, too. *That's all you know.*"

"That's a joke, that's a real joke," my father answered bitterly. She'd really hit him where he lived. But he could do the same to her if he had to. "*You* wouldn't have married an economist, Ida. You wouldn't have known how to pronounce the word. You started loving me when you saw my new car. You can talk against the store but sometimes I think you married the store more than you married me! Well, I'll tell you something: I might be a loser, but where would *you* be without me? How far do you think your fish market voice would get you if you weren't married to someone who owned a big grocery store!"

Same old pattern.

Psychologically, my father may have been marrying his own mother, and my mother may have been marrying the *opposite* of her own father. But when I was five years old, and for a long, long time after, all I knew—all I sensed—was that each of them had made a horrible mistake. Not only for each other. For me. Especially for me.

"God," I used to plead, looking up at the ceiling before going to sleep each night, "Why did you give me the wrong parents? Why?"

My mother, Ida Lefkowitz Burstein, did have a kind heart underneath her lower East Side exterior, yet she kept it so well hidden it might as well not have been there at all. My mother wasn't just a shouter. She was a picker. There was nothing that I seemed to do right. No matter what I did she always seemed to find fault. If I got a tiny speck of dust on my white shoes she would take me upstairs immediately to have them cleaned. Her whole existence seemed to center around cleanliness. When you walked into our living room you almost feared to sit down. Everything was so goddamned perfect you felt as if you were intruding on some photographer snapping his perfect setting for *House Beautiful.*

My mother never paid me compliments. But oh how I needed just one I could believe. Just one! Even when she paid me a compliment, it always seemed left-handed. My mother had a way of scaring me with her compliments. For example: "My Rona is such a pretty girl," she'd tell her friends. "But especially her hair. *Especially* the hair. Have you looked at it close? I could look at it for hours. For *hours.* It's so thick and shiny, Rona's hair. She'll never have to worry about going bald."

Worry about going bald!

What five-year-old would worry about that *unless* her mother kept bringing it up?

She even made it seem like I *would* go bald by telling obvious lies with the compliment. Like, "My little girl is so pretty." Or "My little girl is so neat. If she gets even one spot on her shoe—*one spot*—she'll run right into her room and make it clean again."

I wasn't pretty. I was plain, at best. Ugly, by some standards.

And oh how I wished to be sloppy. I would have given anything to throw my clothes all around and on the floor. But the few times I did so there she was, picking up after me, making me feel more incompetent!

But for all of my longing to be petted and admired, I would never have believed my mother anyway. I didn't have to look into a mirror to know I wasn't beautiful; all I had to do was feel myself. At age nine I was fully developed—and extremely self-conscious. My breasts had grown to such an enormous size that when I walked I looked like the Leaning Tower of Pisa. I was an oddity all right. I bought sweaters five sizes larger than necessary, and once I even thought about cutting my breasts off with a pair of scissors. But I wasn't in the mood for the sight of blood that day, so I put the scissors away and prayed for a new alternative.

At age 9 I also became a real woman, and the knowledge sent Ida into a state of near hysteria.

"Oh, my God, Harry, what are we going to do? Nine's much too young for her to get her period. She knows nothing yet about the facts of life and I certainly don't know what to tell her. Once she saw me putting a sanitary napkin on and asked me what was happening. I tried to tell her that when she gets older she'd be doing the same thing and that when she saw blood I would then tell her all about how babies were made. I never expected it would be when she was nine! . . . And, Harry, what are we going to do if some man should get funny with her and she won't be able to fend for herself? Tell me, Harry. Tell me?"

Ida needn't have worried. I had discovered long ago how babies were made. I found a book in my father's library, and it was extremely explicit.

After the shock of me becoming a woman had faded—it really lasted only a few minutes—Ida again turned her waking hours back to finding a new doctor. She absolutely refused to give up. By now I was fed up. I hated being *shlepped* from one doctor to another; having another doctor put his hands all over me; having another doctor feel my legs, my ass, my arms, my stomach, my breasts. I was fed up. But there was little I could do. When Ida insisted, Ida insisted. I felt helpless and the situation was hopeless. I wasn't old enough yet to leave home and to tell everyone to go to hell.

One day I came home from school to discover my mother smiling and excited. "Guess what?" she blurted out. "I finally got an appointment with the famous Dr. Mayer and his brother. They're supposed to be the greatest doctors in the world on muscle diseases. They said if we come to Syracuse they'll see us. Oh, Rona, isn't that wonderful? I just know the Mayer brothers will know what's wrong with you and be able to fix you up like new."

"But, Ma, I don't want to be fixed up like new. I don't give a damn anymore. Why can't you let me be? Ma, I can't stand going to another doctor again. I'm so sick of being jabbed with needles and being given new pills. I'm tired of being a guinea pig. Please, Ma. Let's not go. Just let me be."

"Not on your life, sweetheart," Ida snapped.

"But it is my life, and you're making a mess of it!"

"A mess of it! Why, you ungrateful little snotnose. How can you say that? Do you know how I've sacrificed for you? Do you know what I've done for you? Do you think it's been easy for your father and me to carry you up on buses and trains and *shlep* you all over the country to try and find out what's wrong with you? How can you say that, Rona?"

"Well, I've said it. And I'm fed up!"

"Don't talk to me like that, Rona. You're showing no respect and I won't take that from you. We're going to Syracuse to see the Mayers and that's that. Do you understand?"

"Yes, I understand. But let me tell you this, Mother. I'm not going to see another doctor after the Mayers even if they tell me I'm going to die! Do you understand that?" And I slammed the bedroom door in my mother's face.

On a Friday morning we left for Syracuse by train. I spent the eight-hour trip staring out the window.

Our appointment with the Mayer doctors was for 8:30 Saturday morning. They didn't usually see patients on the weekend, but Ida had been so persuasive in her many letters, that they finally agreed to see the little girl with the peculiar muscle problems no doctor had been able to diagnose.

The Mayer brothers hospital was very austere and it smelled like every other hospital I had ever been in. Even the examining rooms were the same cubbyholes separated by thin partitions. I often wondered why doctors whispered to my parents. Unless a person was deaf, you could hear everything they had to say.

The examination was extremely extensive. It was in two parts. The first part was like taking a history exam. The doctors asked all kinds of medical questions about Ida and Harry's family backgrounds. They asked me questions about where I ached and what part of me hurt most. When I told them nothing ached and nothing hurt, they looked shocked, surprised, and most of all perturbed. The second half of the examination was strictly physical. The blood tests seemed endless, the X-rays the same. And the tapping of the bones became monotonous. Then for two hours after that the doctors made me sit down and get up; sit down and get up. This was the horrible part, because it was under these circumstances that my handicap became visible. Once I was on the floor there was no way for me to get back on my feet without help unless I could hold on to something for support and lift myself slowly. This required me to call on every muscle capable of doing something. It was not a pretty sight, and I felt I looked like a tub of lard with no place to go. After two hours, I was exhausted and close to the breaking point. It seemed so cruel and ridiculous when one of the doctors asked me to do it just "one more time."

Ida watched from the sidelines with a pained expression in her eyes. She finally blurted out, "I don't think it's necessary again, Doctor. That's all my daughter can do. It won't get any better, probably only worse."

The doctors finally told me to put my clothes back on. Outside the cubbyhole, they told Ida to come back with me in three weeks. Ida asked if there wasn't anything they could surmise now.

"From what I've been able to see, Mrs. Burstein, I have a feeling Rona might have had a twenty-four or forty-eight hour virus—a mild dose of polio—which left her with these handicaps. Of course, I'm not sure yet. It will be very important to examine our X-rays and the blood tests, and my brother and I will have to analyze all the information we've been able to see today. I think it would be wise of you to return in three weeks."

Disappointed, Ida agreed. Three weeks later, on the train back to Syracuse, I was angry with myself. I'd sworn never go back to see another doctor, and here I was going to see those two creeps again. If they made me squat and get up once more, I vowed to myself, I'd kick them where it hurt.

Sure enough, once more they asked me to get on the floor and try to lift myself up. But somehow, I absolutely couldn't; it was as if I were frozen all over and nothing worked. Realizing it was no use, Dr. Mayer lifted me back onto the examining table and told me to be a good girl and get dressed.

I felt sorrier for my mother than I did for myself. I had been learning to live with whatever it was that made me physically unable to do the things other kids could do. I even compensated by becoming an A student. After all, A students don't get bullied. They get respect from other kids, because dumb kids need them to help them cheat on exams.

The Mayers had taken my mother into the next room. I thought I was being cute when I put my ear to the wall. I heard one of the Mayers say, "Sit down, Mrs. Burstein." A chair moved and I presumed my mother did what the doctor asked.

"My brother and I are not quite sure how to tell you this, but since I'm sure you'd want to know the truth, here it is. My brother and I are convinced Rona has a deteriorating muscle disease—not acquired but congenital—and it's getting worse. It's hard to say how much longer she'll live. We guess not more than a few years!"

My mother gasped!

I gasped, too! I pulled away from the wall and covered my ears with my hands. "No! No! No! I'm not going to die. Those doctors are crazy. Famous people don't die young and I'm not going to die because someday I'm going to be famous! I'm not! I'm not! I'm *not!*"

I sobbed so loudly that Ida and the doctors ran into the room. I was on the floor beating my fists, my head against the wall. "Do you hear me? I'm not going to die!"

They hadn't suspected I could hear them. My mother lifted me off the floor and held me tightly. We both cried bitterly. I was the first to regain composure.

"Let's go, Ma. Don't cry. I'm not going to die. They're crazy. You'll see. I'll be all better. Let's go."

After the Mayer brothers, I was even more determined

to show them all—every single one of them who had ever pointed a finger at me—I'd be bigger and better than any one of them, so help me God, I would. How I would do it, I had no idea. But if God had willed me to be the daughter of the Bursteins, whom I did not want as parents, then He would show me the way to get out. Now, only to keep the faith.

My mother made one last attempt. Upon our return from Syracuse she learned of a new muscle-disease research center at the famed New York Hospital. She made an appointment. I refused to go.

"How many times do I have to tell you, Ma, I'm not going to any more doctors, hospitals, or what have you? I told you once and I'm telling you again. I'm not going to die. Do you hear me? And I'm not going to get poked again by any doctor or injected again with any kind of new serum or take any kind of new pills."

But all of my ultimatums were in vain. Ida dragged me to New York Hospital, where we waited for what seemed like an eternity to meet with the chief doctor in charge of muscle diseases. Dr. Milhorat was extremely interested in my case. After the usual extensive examination, his diagnosis was that I indeed had a muscular problem, and there was no name for it. For the time being, he would call it dystrophy, but unlike the Mayer brothers he did not think I was dying. For the next four years I was his number one guinea pig. Every kind of new serum or pill which was perfected for human consumption was tested on me; and, as he had suspected, nothing changed. Well, practically nothing. I still had difficulty climbing stairs or performing any function which required the use of my limbs in anything but a walking or sitting state. However, my determination to make those muscles work or to find substitute muscles was so overwhelming, Dr. Milhorat suspected his days with me were numbered. And he was right. Somewhere between my thirteenth and fourteenth birthdays, I rebelled, and it could be heard from one end of Queens to another. It concluded with a vicious fight between mother and daughter that I would remember forever.

We were standing in the narrow hallway separating the sleeping area from the living area of our apartment. Another Thursday had come and gone and it was time again for me to see Dr. Milhorat. I was now seeing him three times a week, and the visits were beginning to interfere with my life—at least, the life I was planning to begin as soon as I could get free.

I don't know who started the fight, but it began with my mother's nagging. Suddenly, everything I said or did was wrong.

"My God, Rona, can't you move faster than that?"

"If I could move faster, Mama, you wouldn't be taking me to the doctor, would you?"

"You know I didn't mean it sarcastically. Now hurry, we've got to pick up some things before we see Dr. Milhorat."

"Right, Mother. A sarcastic person couldn't devote her whole life to being a do-gooder for her daughter!"

"Don't you start that again, Rona Burstein. I won't have you and your father talking that way about me. That's the one thing I won't have. I only want that you should be made well and happy—"

"*Mother,* if you want to make me *happy,* let me *alone.*"

"Get dressed, Rona."

"No."

"Rona. I said *get dressed.*"

"I said *no*."

My mother took my blouse and tossed it over at me. "Put this on."

I caught it and threw it back at her. It fell to the floor.

"Don't push me, my daughter."

"Like you push me every minute of my life, except when I'm sleeping!"

She picked up the blouse and walked over to me with it, held it out. "Put . . . this . . . *on!*"

I let the blouse drop to the floor.

"I'll drag you, Rona. I'll drag you like I dragged you a year ago. Like I dragged you the first time. I'll do whatever I have to do to get you there."

"Drag."

"What?"

"I said drag. Drag me, Mama. *If you can.*"

"Of course I can!"

"We'll see. I weigh more than you now, you know. *I am* crippled, it's true, but that might be an advantage if I use it properly. I'm taller than you, too. And I'll tell you what, Mama; for once I think I am finally more determined than even you are."

My mother put her hand on my arm just as she had a year ago. Almost nonchalantly, I dropped into a heap on the floor. "You can begin by lifting me, Mama."

She couldn't. She tugged. She pulled. She grunted. She shouted. She even cursed. But she couldn't.

She took a breath finally, stopped, stood up straight a step or so back from me.

"What is this all about, Rona?"

"The same thing as usual, Mama, only this time *I mean it*. You see, Mother dear, I'm really *not* a cripple. *You* are the cripple."

"You're talking crazy," she began to say, but the words caught in her throat. I sensed in that instant that the balance had at last shifted, that we were now on the level of ideas, not brute force, that *my* idea was stronger, and that if I only stuck to it I could win. And somehow, it would mean I'd have beaten her for good. "That's right, Mama, you don't know what I'm talking about, do you? Unless someone talks to you about a recipe or gossips about a person in the family, you don't know from nothing. Anything else but *that* kind of talk is for me and my father, right? We're the ones who read books and have our heads filled with ideas, and books and ideas aren't practical, are they? Practical is all you know. And what could be more practical than *shlepping* your daughter to doctors your whole life so that she doesn't have to be a poor cripple anymore? What makes more sense than *that?* Except that it doesn't make sense, Mama, unless someone understands the *idea* behind it. Unless someone understands that you just don't want me to grow up, crippled or not. And do you know why? Because my being a cripple—"

"You're *not* a cripple. Don't use that word or I'll smack you!"

"I *am* a cripple, Mama. Maybe I'll always be a cripple. But don't worry about it—unless you *want* to worry about it. Unless *you're* the cripple like I said. Because that's what's behind it all. I can see it. I see it now! Miserable. You are a miserable human being. You've always been miserable. You thought Daddy could make you feel better because he had a roadster and owned a grocery store, but it didn't work. You thought children would make you feel better. But it didn't work. And then to have a cripple! That made you even *more* miserable. Except that you love it. Beneath it all you *love it*. Because you are simply a miserable human being and . . . you . . . need . . . an . . . excuse . . . for . . . it. Well, I'm sick and tired of being your excuse!"

She did smack me then, with all her might across the side of my face.

It jarred me, but before she could do anything else, I grabbed her hand with mine, grabbed her hair with my other hand and pulled myself up off the floor. Crazed, I threw her against the wall with all *my* might . . . and began banging her head against it.

She quit.

"Rona," she said in a rare whisper, "I'll never speak to you again as long as I live. I promise you that."

"Good. Don't! I hope you die now!" I got out of the house, filled with rage. "Oh, God," I screamed as I got to the street. "Get me out of here!"

CHAPTER FOUR

Eddie Fisher was the most handsome thing I'd ever laid eyes on. I had seen him at a hotel in the Catskills that summer. He was a singer, not too famous yet, but destined for enormous stardom. I just sensed it. Maybe I could help him become famous? I had learned that Fisher's manager had an office in Manhattan. I walked toward the elevated trains. My mother had never allowed me to take the train by myself. After all, how was I going to climb the stairs without my mother's help? *Cripple!* How was I going to do anything without my mother's help? *Cripple!*

My head was pounding when I got to the station. My temples were throbbing. *Can I be having a stroke? No, I said to myself, no one has a stroke at thirteen. I can't be having a stroke.* I looked at the steps. There were a lot more than the thirty-two I had become used to at P.S. 5. And now at junior high I didn't have to worry. There were only ten small steps to the first landing and then there was an elevator. Elevators. What a great blessing. God bless Mr. Otis, I mused, trying to calm myself. *Why doesn't the el have an elevator?* Staring at the four flights of steps in front of me, I felt frozen. My feet refused to move. There were so many people walking up and down. What would they say when they saw me? I thought I would die on the spot if anyone asked me if I needed help, but it was now or never. Looking around for a last time, I took a deep breath, grabbed hold of the bannister and slowly began pulling myself up the stairs, one at a time. I didn't give a damn who looked. Over in Manhattan I knew there was freedom, and if I ached with embarrassment for the way I climbed stairs, in the end it wouldn't matter anyway. I just kept climbing. Some of the people did stare and then I was at the turnstile. I found two dimes in my purse, leftover lunch money. It would be enough to get me to 57th Street and back. I put the dime in the slot, looked at the two more flights I had to climb, prayed to God He'd give me the strength to do it, took another deep breath, and up I went. The train was coming. Soon I would be free.

At home, in the privacy of my room, I had practiced trying to get in and out of a chair without looking awkward. I knew it wasn't going to be easy, but I just *had* to do it. I couldn't afford to have train doors close in my face because I wasn't able to get out of my seat in time. Up and down I would go until every muscle in my back and thighs would ache so painfully I'd be ready to cry.

And now the time had come. The first test was about to begin.

I mentally reconstructed the subway route from the times I had traveled with my mother and recalled that the second or third station coming out of the tunnel was 57th Street. That had to be my stop.

The conductor yelled, "57th Street, neeeext!"

I had taken the window side because if I put one hand carefully on the windowsill and the other underneath me, I could brace myself for the lift out. Unfortunately, I hadn't counted on a big heavyset black man, who looked as if he should be nine months pregnant, squeezing himself in beside me. I wondered how I could get him to move just a bit without having to explain, in detail, my physical problem.

My grandmother Lefkowitz once told me, "Rona, just use your eyes. They're so expressive, so revealing. Only a fool won't be able to tell what's on your mind!"

But the man didn't budge no matter how mournfully I batted my lashes. I started squirming; he moved an inch; I braced my hand on the sill and then it was all over. The doors flew open and I was standing on the platform along with fifty or more people hurriedly moving in several directions.

I was telling myself, "Well, that wasn't too bad," when it dawned on me that the ordeal was far from over. Ahead of me was a gargantuan staircase that looked never-ending, and again I found myself looking heavenward and asking silently, "Are You sure You couldn't have made all stairs escalators? Do You realize, if You had, no one would ever know there was anything wrong with my legs?" But there was no answer from God.

The sign above me indicated 55th Street was to the left and 57th Street was to the right. I was standing close to the 57th Street exit, but I figured if I walked the length of the platform in the other direction, by the time I got there the crowd would have thinned out. Hopefully, I could make it to the first landing before the next train would pull in.

It worked. By the time I reached the 55th Street side most everyone had disappeared. Two middle-aged women, not too different from my mother, passed me, an inquiring, helpful look on their faces. I stared back coldly at them and they looked away. A tall man who reminded me of one of the Mayer brothers paused ever so slightly

on his way down. I held my head up and took a step.
With both hands on the railing I lifted myself to the next
step . . . and then the next . . . At last I saw the sun's
light and I smiled and chuckled to myself, "I did it! I
did it!" And then I thought about my mother and wondered if Mama would ever believe I had gone to New York
City, on a subway, all by myself. I decided the best thing
I could do was to bring home some proof. Then again,
maybe my mother would keep her promise and never talk
to me again.

Out on 55th Street, I was greeted by a warm blast of
air up my skirt as I passed over the subway grate. It was
so hot out even a warm draft was better than no draft
at all.

Number 221 West 57th Street was just twelve stories
high, an old building whose small entry looked like it had
been slightly face-lifted. The entry walls were maroon
marble and the floors were cream-colored marble with
maroon trim. The newly painted but wheezing elevator
completed the picture. The building was antiquity, not
elegance. But it was okay, I thought to myself. *It's okay.
This is just where I should begin.*

I walked out of the elevator on the ninth floor and
came face to face with the receptionist, who was so busy
at the switchboard that she hardly noticed me. "Gdafternoon, Milton Blackstone. . . . Gdafternoon, Blackstone.
. . . Oh, yeah. Who are ya? . . . Gdafternoon, Milton
Blackstone. . . . Just a minute, girlie," she said to me
without looking up.

My eyes wandered everywhere. Life-size posters of
famous people covered the walls. I recognized every one
of them. Especially, my Eddie Fisher.

"Who'd ya say ya wantedasee, girlie?" the receptionist
broke in.

"Oh. I didn't. But my name's Rona Burst—I mean, Rona *Barrett*." Without having given it a second's thought, I had changed my name. I'd known Burstein would never make it in the world of glamour. Burstein was for the grocery business. "I understand Mr. Blackstone handles a very talented actor-singer named Eddie Fisher. I think I can be of some value to him."

"How old are ya, honey?"

"I'll be fourteen."

"Does your mother know . . . Milton Blackstone, Gdafternoon . . . what you're up to?"

"I'm an almost-fourteen." I was surprising myself that I was able to keep up with her.

"How can ya be of what you call value?"

"I want to start a fan club for him."

I knew *that* was something I should save for Mr. Blackstone. "What's *your* name?" I asked. "It's hard to talk to someone when you don't know their name."

"Dottie," she answered. "Gdafternoon, Milton Blackstone. . . . Who? Doesn't work here anymore. . . . Gdafternoon, Blackstone. . . . Hold on. . . . Dottie Gallagher, Barrett. Been here fifteen years. Wouldn't think so, would ya? I was *sixteen*. Mr. Blackstone's an all right helluva guy. Shy, real quiet except when he's hot about something one way or the other, but tries to be fair. Pays a great bonus at Christmas. He *has* to—to make up for the other fifty-one weeks!" She laughed with that infectious quality that only the Irish have. "But . . . Milton Blackstone . . . Gdafternoon. . . . He's talking, can you wait? . . . It comes in handy. Just a couple of months away now. Doesn't seem important, but it all adds up, Barrett. With prices going up every day. Besides, only have to transfer once on the subway. Gotta think about things like carfare, Barrett. What'd ya say your first name was?"

I said my new name again.

It gave me gooseflesh.

I was beginning to be new.

I didn't get to Milton Blackstone that day, but Dottie finally did usher me into the office of George Bennett. He was Blackstone's right-hand man. I told him why I was there. I believed that Eddie Fisher must have an invisible but solid following. Solid because almost anyone who'd seen him, as I had, would be overwhelmed by his talent and boyish charisma. But invisible because no one had let them know that *we* knew they existed and that there *were* so many of them.

"How do you know there *are?*" he asked me. "I think the kid is a good talent and it's pretty clear that you think he's the greatest thing that ever walked on ten toes, but how can you be sure about the rest of the world?"

"If I'm wrong, you have nothing to lose. But if I'm right," I said, "it could make a big difference for him and for Mr. Blackstone."

And for—He pointed his finger at me.

I nodded openly. I wasn't there to do a good deed, although I did want to see Eddie Fisher become a star almost more than anything else in the world. But I couldn't separate that from *how* he'd become one. Until that time, there really were no such things as fan clubs. There were loosely organized followers or worshippers or admirers of certain stars and entertainers. Possibly they even corresponded with each other or all got together once in a while when the performer came to town. My idea was to have them in constant touch with each other, to have them feel like a political organization, to find recruits, to have activities, to have membership cards and get news-letters every week, to take action in their local areas with the disk jockeys and the talent bookers so that their man's name would spread, his records would sell in the millions, television stations would almost *have* to put him on because of the letters they'd get, record stores would be acutely aware that he was the biggest thing on the horizon, and so on and so on and so on until Eddie Fisher *became* the biggest star in the whole world!

"You don't talk about him like it's publicity," George said when I stopped to catch my breath. "You talk about him like it's a cause. I never heard of anything in this business on such a grand scale."

"Look, George," I said, using his first name, "what have you got to lose?" I was drawing on what I'd learned from my father. "Even if it fails, you'll know what *can't* be done. But I say it *can*."

"You're a cracker, kid," he said when I'd finished my speech. "You never even met Eddie."

"*Seeing* him once is all I needed. He's going to be a big star. Maybe the biggest of all of them, bigger than any of those pictures you've got on the wall of your reception room. I can help it to happen faster, I really can."

He scratched his greying hair like there were fleas in it and smiled wide. "You know, I bet you could. I really bet you could."

He was through thinking it over. But I could see something was getting in his way. "Look," I said. "If *you* think I *can* and *I* know I can, what's stopping us?"

He scratched his head a few more times. "Your name. I go by two things. If the talk fits the face. If the name fits the face. A person's like a puzzle, you know. I've got to feel it fits. Your name doesn't fit. You don't look like a Barrett. Dottie out there—*she* could be a Barrett. And Rona. What's with *Rona?* I think I only heard it once before in my entire thirty-seven years, you know?"

"Did you expect the president of the Eddie Fisher fan clubs to be ordinary? When I was born, there were just twelve Ronas in the whole United States. And Barrett— well, it's my name. *Now.*"

"What do you mean *now,* Rona? When wasn't it?"

I underplayed for all I was worth. If I wanted to prove I could promote performers, I'd better be a performer myself. Besides, *my* "act" was from the heart.

"Twenty minutes ago," I said coolly.

George Bennett stared at me. For what seemed like minutes but was only seconds, he didn't move a muscle. Then he broke up. "Rona Barrett, you're a cracker!" he said.

"By the way," I added, "you should change *your* name, too. You don't look like a George."

His face became serious. For a space there it was as if he was a child again, and I was the much older one. "You know," he spoke softly, "funny you should say that. Funny. I never liked my name. Bennett I like. It fits, right?" I nodded. "Yeah, Bennett fits. But not George. I'm no George." He scratched his head more slowly. "What would you say I *am,* Rona?"

"A . . . Brett!"

Suddenly, in a more theatrical gesture than I thought he was capable of, George went down on one knee before me. "Scarlet!"

"I said Brett, not Rhett!"

He got up. "Brett . . . maybe I *will* change it. Sometime maybe I will. . . . You know, kid, what you say just might be true. About your fan clubs. Every day we have so many letters from gals wanting to start things just like that, and for Eddie too, that we hired a couple of girls to at least answer the mail. Anyway, with enthusiasm and *chutzpah* like yours, who am I to deny a kid a chance? I'll tell you what . . ."

I got the job.

George put me to work immediately. He first gave me the desk right next to his and let me go through all the mail. "Here," he said, almost tossing it in piles from his desk to mine. "See if you can get these thousands of girls to do what you say they'll do."

There was no talk of actual salary, but I knew he would eventually pay me if I succeeded. At the moment the pay was "all the coffee and coke you can drink, free postage, and stationery. And I'll have you driven home. I don't want any mother thinking I have abducted her almost-fourteen-year-old daughter."

I almost wished that George had thoughts of abducting me. It wasn't just that he was handsome in a Brett kind of manner. It was that no boy, no man, had ever looked at me in that "you're pretty" way. Maybe they never would in my whole life. But maybe if I made Eddie Fisher famous, just possibly *he* might look at me as a woman.

I didn't let it matter too much. *So I'm not pretty,* I thought. *So I'm not rich and I'm working for nothing. But I do have a brain. I'll show them I have the best brain they've ever seen. Maybe God did me a fair turn after all. Maybe He gave me a special way to think to make up for the way I can't physically do things like other people.*

I dug in and started opening the letters.

At dinnertime that night, I had a good feeling inside myself. For the first time as long as I could remember, possibly in my whole life, I had had an entire day from beginning to end that had been good.

When I walked into the house, my mother was talking to me again. She was furious, wanted to know where I was. I handled her.

At that moment, I thought I could handle anything.

The three-month "trial" period passed at Milton Black-stone Agency. George never even mentioned it to me, and I never brought it up, just went right on working. After school four hours. And, of course, dozens of hours on weekends on my own. The results began to trickle in, then flow in—with the hint of a flood in the future.

There was already a flood from my mother. She couldn't get over the fact that her little baby was taking a subway train five days a week without *her*.

"Don't worry, Ida," my father would say to her at night, "Rona's just going through a *meshugunah* phase. Eddie Fisher! Show business! She's a kid. She's *thirteen years old*. Let her alone. Better she goes to work than gets in trouble with boys."

"Get in trouble with *boys!*" my mother would shriek. "Boys! Huh!"

My parents' preoccupation with sex bugged me. Oh, I knew the facts of life, but they didn't apply to Rona Barrett.

My parents didn't know that my love affair with Eddie would be just like in the movies. How I loved the movies! They were really my *other* love in life, besides Eddie Fisher. I'd go every chance I could. Two theaters in my neighborhood only changed shows twice weekly. That meant I could only see four movies every week plus Saturday matinees where there'd be an extra showing of Hopalong Cassidy or Charlie Chan.

Sometimes if I really loved a picture, I'd go back two

or three times if it were possible. Shirley Temple was one of my favorites. My father had been taking me to see her films since I was nine months old. Like me, she had apple cheeks, but the world loved her for it. Of course, her shapely legs could dance up and down the stairs like lights blinking on and off.

Elizabeth Taylor was my very favorite, though. She was so beautiful in *National Velvet.* God, she was gorgeous. Those purple velvet eyes. The first time I saw the film, I spent every waking moment staring into the mirror in our apartment wondering if there would ever be a way *I* could look like that. Finally, I realized that I couldn't change my eyes, but *maybe* I could do something with my nose. I sat playing with it, holding it this way, turning it that, covering it up just the right amount, thinking of what Eddie Fisher would feel when he saw it the new way. Like Elizabeth Taylor's.

Because that's what my love with him would be like. As it was in the movies. My parents were preoccupied with sex, my girlfriends were finally getting their periods, going on dates and making out, but I saw Eddie smothering me with kisses until I fell off to sleep, whispering the same kind of words to me that he shouted out so tenderly and poignantly in his songs.

Everything good that ever happened for me in my life began for me in a "dream" when I lay alone in my bed at night. If I pictured it like that long enough and hard enough, one day the dream and reality would fuse, like one scene to another with that special Hollywood photography. What I did for him would become what he would do for me. It would be pure and floating and beautiful. I closed my eyes and made the mental picture of it exactly how I wanted it to be between us. Now and then the picture wasn't too clear, so I squeezed my eyes a little tighter, concentrated harder, until finally the image emerged as precise as one of those expensive picture post-cards you buy in the Empire State Building.

First, there was the setting. Then I put Eddie into it, just as I put Milton Blackstone into it before I went for the job. I left out everything else, only what we'd say to one another. If someone said something wrong, I'd erase it, erase the whole picture, begin over again until it went exactly right. Sometimes I'd have to do it dozens and dozens and possibly hundreds of times before it was per-fect. But I always did get it perfect in my head, and, once it was perfect there, it would happen in real life. Going to work for Milton Blackstone wasn't the first time I'd done that. It was merely the first time I'd been aware of "picturing" while I was doing it. I'd actually begun years before, seeing myself not crippled someday.

Once the picture was finally perfect, I could bring it back whenever I wanted to just by closing my eyes. It was like having your own movie theater inside your head where you could show your favorite picture at a blink.

But it was going to be a little difficult for Eddie to sweep me off my feet if he touched me and I literally fell to the floor and wasn't able to get up.

More than ever, therefore, I practiced and devised ways to make up for my disability. If there were a chair or desk around, of course, I'd learned to make it back up almost casually. And I had a dozen lines prepared as to why I'd fallen. For a while I'd lean on one knee, place my hands in front of me on the floor, bracing myself against it and lifted myself into a position where both knees finally locked. That way I could sometimes lift the upper half of my torso.

Sometimes.

I couldn't take a chance on *sometimes* with Eddie.

So I devised an entirely original way of getting up. It was good enough, in fact, that my sister—stricken with the same, evidently genetic, ailment—was able to learn it within a few months. So she not only had a way of overcoming the terrible embarrassment I'd gone through, but it strengthened her legs so that by the time she was my age, she had hardly any noticeable problem at all.

What I did was to get on one knee, locking it in position and, using that leg as a kind of pivot, actually swing myself up. At first I looked like a dog on all fours with her rear end sticking in the air.

It appeared so grotesque, there wasn't a reason in the world I could give myself for wanting anyone else to see it. Anything I could do to avoid being placed in that position became my prime concern, and as a result, I became careful to keep myself in very safe scenes. I would discover later on in life that this contributed to my avoidance of ever loving or being loved completely. If loving meant someone seeing you as a monster and then turning away as all people do when they view monsters, you must not allow the monster to appear.

But after a while, as I got stronger, I was able to give a certain grace to the maneuver. I will say that if I've ever learned *anything* in this life, it's how to pull myself up by my own bootstraps.

It happened one Saturday.

. . . He was sitting on my desk when I came through the door. I was wearing a short skirt; my legs were my best feature, ironic as that was. On my desk was the deluge of mail for him that had begun to come in as a result of my efforts. Yes, I was still plain, ugly to some. Still fat. Still crippled, though *he* wouldn't know *that*. But I *had something*. He'd see it. Eddie Fisher would see that same quality *he* had, that childlike I-can-overcome-anything-and-sing-of-it-louder-than-anyone feeling, and *that* would overcome what I looked like!

Because I'd poured all that feeling into making *him* a *star*. Already he had more and better bookings; local record stations were spinning his records more (and in other cities, too, if the reports were right that I'd received from local fan club presidents); he'd gotten several variety show appearances; and I had a big demonstration, long before they were in style politically, planned for spring when he played the Copa.

"I've been waiting for you for hours, Rona," he said. "Waiting for you for weeks, in fact. Couldn't *wait* to meet you, meet the gal who's doing so much for me. Can't thank you enough."

He planted a kiss on my cheek. It was a show biz kiss, but it was warm, and didn't he linger there an instant longer than he had to?

"I really wanted to meet you before this, Rona, but you know how Milt's had me on the road promoting the new record." Then, glancing around, to make sure he wasn't upsetting the office, Eddie planted a softer, longer kiss.

On my lips.

"Would you mind if I drove you home after work today? Maybe we could have a bit of dinner and talk about the *future*."

Anyone listening would have thought he meant his own future, his career. But the word had something extra to it—just as when he sang. It meant *our* future.

Dinnertime was only two hours away, but that was a

lifetime. Finally, *finally,* I was walking into the elevator and out of the building. With *him*. He instinctively walked slower with me than he did with other people, as if he sensed that it would make us look just right together, the perfect couple, my affliction not existing at all!

The next few hours passed like minutes, *seconds*. He whirlwinded me through dinner at a dark, intimate little place, and from there we drove to the farthest tip of Long Island, parked, and watched the ocean break upon the shore. When he kissed me for the third time, it had all the passion and turbulence of the huge waves themselves. He put his arms around me, pulled me close. For a fleeting second, I wondered how many other girls he'd done this with, possibly at this very place. Yet I *knew* that we had more between us already than he could have had with any of them, knew it because he'd seen past my fat, apple-cheeked face and overweight, slow-moving body to what was *inside* me. Because the same thing was inside him. But, as if in answer to my very thoughts, Eddie said, "Rona, I've been with other girls. Girls who are going to become movie stars. Girls the world would say I'd be crazy not to spend my time with. But already, I'm so crazy about you I can't think about them. No kidding. Sure, I care what you've done for me. I won't say that's not part of it. But it's that *you* did what no one else was able to, that *you* understand how important becoming famous is to me. To be Number One. To be at the top. The pinnacle . . ."

It was like a fantasy. . . .

It *was* a fantasy, tough reader. It never happened.

Eddie Fisher was as much into apple-cheeked, fat-bodied chicks as Hitler was into the B'nai B'rith.

As a matter of fact, Jewish girls were one of Eddie's

hangups. He hated them with a passion. I remember
the time I knew him for what he was once and for all.
He was sitting on Dottie's desk in the Blackstone office,
just a few feet from me, thumbing through a fan magazine
that had a story on him. He'd never once thanked me
for anything I'd done. He'd breezed in and out of the office
usually without as much as a hello, and never a good-bye.
And as for loving me, it was a question as to whether
Eddie was capable of love at all. He was blinder than
Ray Charles when it came to seeing past the skin.

His latest female acquisition was a show-girl redhead
with body and features so perfect you'd think she'd been
manufactured by Mannikins, Inc.

But even if Eddie hadn't been so strictly superficial in
the way he chose, his strong beliefs would have
stopped him dead in his tracks every time he came face
to face with a nose that wasn't pugged. When I eventually
took the chance and asked him about it, he just kept
skimming the magazine—like he skimmed life.

"Jewish girls are *nudges,*" he at last said without looking
up. "I wouldn't date a Jewish broad if my life depended
on it. Not even if my career depended on it!" He found
something in the magazine that interested him and
stopped talking for a minute.

"Why?" I asked quietly.

"Why! Isn't it obvious?" he said, after finishing the
paragraph he was reading. "For one thing, they think
they're doing you a big favor when it comes to the sex
department. They always make you feel guilty that you
made them do something they didn't want to do. That
means the next time you'd better buy them a big bauble
to make up for what they should have been doing naturally! I've seen it happen a million times. Before you know

it, you've got a depleted bank account because this Jewish broad has bribed you into buying every goddamned new-fangled goody in the world just to get a piece of ass. The *goyishe* dames are different. They're always happy to do it. No questions asked, either. And if *you* happen to give *them* something extra in the sex department, they buy *you* presents!"

I simply couldn't take it. I wouldn't risk coming right out and arguing with him, but I couldn't let him be *so* wrong without knowing it. "Maybe some Jewish girls are like that. Maybe even most, Eddie. I don't know. But not *all* Jewish girls are like that. *I know.*"

He looked at me with astonishment. "I wasn't talking about *you*," he said. "I'm talking about Jewish girls I might *date*."

I couldn't talk. I sunk low in my chair, hating the hard wood of it, because all I wanted was to go down, down, out of sight. *If only I were taller,* I kept thinking. *If I could just stretch myself . . . lose the fat . . . the cheeks . . . change the nose . . . walk like those girls he dated, like striding colts. . . . If only I could change the outside enough so that he'd notice me, and then I could make him see the inside, get to his inside, the soul that must be there or else he couldn't sing like he did, look like he did. . . .*

But no way, José.

Eddie was young, but in some ways his ideas were cast in bronze. "If I were going to get married, maybe, *maybe,* I say," he encored. "My old man told me Jewish broads make the best mothers, and you can stick to gentiles for fucking as extracurricular activities. But I'm not ready for marriage. No sir!"

Shutting up took almost as much self-discipline as

walking up the four flights to the subway every day. But
I did it. I sat back up in my chair and acted like I hadn't
heard; said, "Did you say something, Ed?"

"Yeah, I said Jewish girls were no good for fucking."

"Yeah, maybe you're right. You're right about just
about everything. That's why I love working for you."

I left the office hurriedly then. It was the first time
I'd ever quit work early. As soon as I was outside the
building, tears began streaming down my face.

By the time I'd reached the subway, I'd dried them.

All I had to do was go home that night, make the whole
picture perfect in my mind again, except *without* Eddie
Fisher. *He* wouldn't fit anymore. *Someone* would. It
wasn't important who they were. It was important that
they'd fit in. To the picture. It was the *picture,* not even
the person. My life was built around that picture.

As I waited for the subway train, I won't say that I
didn't feel like crying again. But one part of me told me
that I'd never cry for Eddie Fisher again . . . even if the
U.S. Army took him out of special services, put him on
active duty, and he died at war.

No, he'd never put his lips on mine, he'd never touch
my hand as a man touches a woman, he'd never even said
an affectionate word, not one word. But I would still be
paid in full for pushing him toward the pinnacle.

Because by getting Eddie Fisher closer to the promised
land, I had gotten Rona Barrett closer, too.

I went to bed early the next nights, so I could lie awake
for hours forming the new picture in my mind. I stared
into the darkness, closing my eyes to blot out even the
dark, until Eddie Fisher was finally removed and the stage
was set for someone new. Oh, Eddie would catapult into
the picture occasionally; my feelings toward him were still

tremendously strong. But they were fantasy feelings, not feelings for *him*.

And I was determined to make my fantasies come true.

Steve Lawrence became my next fantasy. I'd seen Sidney Liebowitz a year earlier at an Interborough Talent Scout Meet before he'd changed his name. He'd won. Because of that, he'd gotten a spot on Arthur Godfrey's Talent Scouts.

Since then, he'd been struggling to make it, like about five thousand other very young male singers across America (and in New York particularly) who'd won some inter-something, gotten on Talent Scouts or a comparable show, and then, when they thought everything would be clear sailing from there on, found that the struggle had just begun. Interborough and even Talent Scouts was like the high school of show business. From it you had to go to college. There were a lot of dropouts in between. Even if you graduated college, there was a Master's and a Ph.D. to get. Then and only then did you have your chance.

The following Friday, I resigned my position as Chief Coordinator for Eddie Fisher Fan Clubs and walked the ten blocks to King Records.

The new picture in my head had been right. Steve himself was in the office, and he liked me immediately. Really liked *me*. I didn't mince words. I told him what I would like to do for him, and that I knew how to do it better than anyone else after working for Eddie Fisher. With a look that Eddie never had on his face in his whole life—though he very often *tried* to look like that—Steve opened his eyes wide like a kid who had seen his first candy store.

"You mean you're giving up Eddie Fisher for *me?*"

"Why not?" I answered matter-of-factly. "You're going

to make it bigger than he is. You might be the next Sinatra."

He lit up like a Christmas tree. "I *want* to be! Oh, I *want* to be! But bigger than Eddie Fisher—"

Then and there I saw Steve's entire personality as clearly as I ever would. On the one hand, he *wanted* to be the biggest. On the other hand, he really didn't *see* himself as the biggest. But I did.

"Steve," I asked him. "Which is bigger? A baby eagle or a giant crow?"

He began laughing. His beautiful blue eyes flashed with pride. He invited me to go home that night to Brooklyn with him to have dinner with his family.

The dinner went superbly. Steve's parents liked me almost more than he did. And why shouldn't they? I had as much faith in his talent as they, and I could help him more because of what I'd done for Eddie. As a matter of fact, they were a little star-struck by me! Eddie Fisher happened to be Mrs. Liebowitz's idol.

For the first time in my life, *I* felt like a celebrity.

I loved it.

My relationship with Steve got deeper and deeper. After school now, instead of going to 57th Street, I went two stations down to 41st and every afternoon sat in front of a typewriter trying to convince radio stations, booking agents, and, above all, the members of the Eddie Fisher Fan Clubs, that Steve Lawrence was the *new* Eddie Fisher. While Steve's agent was trying to book him for TV interviews and club dates, I was booking him for personal appearances in front of two-hundred or three-hundred girls at a time, as well as bugging radio stations to play his latest record. One fed the other. Spurred by my new "cause," of having Steve outdo Eddie, in a matter of months, Steve Lawrence had one of the greatest fan-club networks in the country, blossoming in almost every important city. A huge amount of the membership used to be Eddie Fisher fans.

And this time it was paying off *double*. Because Steve really seemed to care for me.

No, he hadn't asked me to marry him. But I was only fifteen years old! And he did ask my advice about everything. He didn't make a move without talking to what he called "my right arm—the pretty arm." There was only one thing that kept disturbing me. The advice Steve took from me—and the majority of the time, he did take it—was mainly when we talked right before he had to make the decision. If it was something that was a week or two away, often as not he'd end up doing the opposite. Not that I wanted him to be a puppet. Sometimes he was right and I was wrong. But what I was beginning to see was that Steve *was* a puppet—for whomever talked to him last.

So, O.K. He wasn't perfect. But he was pretty close, and if I could make the picture just right in my mind, couldn't I fit that one last piece in later? I'd make him strong, make him see his weakness, after we were married. The important thing was that I became Steve Lawrence's wife, the wife of a *somebody*. And once he was mine, *I'd* be the last one he'd talk to.

I think if I'd genuinely seen Steve's weakness—weakness for *me*, anyway—before I'd fallen in love with him, I'd never have fallen. But that was like Butch Cassidy saying in frustration, after the president of the railroad had hired the six best guns in the U. S. to run him and Sundance Kid out of the country, "If he'd just pay *me* what he's paying *them* to stop *me* from robbing him, I'd stop robbing him!" In other words, if you build the person around the picture, you're in love with the person before you really know him.

But even *that* would have been all right if only Steve had become mine!

Needless to say, he didn't.

And for good reason. At the bottom line, Eydie Gorme was right for Steve. The fantasy of Steve and Rona was mainly in Rona's head. But the fantasy of Steve and Eydie was no fantasy, at least in the beginning. She did more for his career than I ever could, in the one way that I never could: singing with him. If you've got a really good product, promotion will put it over. But if you can make the product *so* good that it's unique, and it's what people want at that time, you hardly need any promotion at all. It puts itself over. It's almost automatic—like a Bette Midler or a *Jonathan Livingston Seagull.* Of course, that kind of thing is rare in show business or politics, let alone any field. Which is why even those at the top want every bit of publicity and promotion that they can get.

But when Steve Lawrence and Eydie Gorme sang together, it *was* instant success. The first time they did it together on the old Steve Allen Show, the whole trade was buzzing about them the next day, to say nothing of the public. *Variety, Cashbox, Record World,* and all the rest called them absolute dynamite!

The following day, a less world-changing but juicier tidbit made its way around the trade: That the sparks Steve and Eydie gave off when they sang to each other were as dynamite as the notes they hit. It did change one world.

Mine.

Now Eydie was the last person Steve talked to. And she was no shrinking violet. I didn't fault her for that.

For the first time in my life, I thought of making what for me was the ultimate aggressive move.

Giving myself to Steve sexually.

For weeks, I was in conflict about whether or not to do it. I wasn't being unrealistic. It would probably do the trick. What nice Jewish boy wouldn't marry a nice Jewish girl he *devirginized?*

I knew that time was getting short. I had to *fish or cut bait.* One Saturday night I went straight to bed and tried to form the picture in my mind. I couldn't. I tried harder. I concentrated as I never had before. I saw myself getting Steve alone where no one could bother us. We'd been in situations like that dozens of times. It would be easy. And he would be easy to influence. Steve was so reactive. He'd make love to me and afterward . . .

At about three in the morning, I almost had it right! I convinced myself that he wouldn't be marrying me just out of duty, that I'd only be bringing the love *out* in him, that I'd be better for Steve than Eydie, a dozen other things. I saw him kissing me, parked in his car near the ocean somewhere, and the kisses were no longer the kind I fantasized with Eddie. They went everywhere, but in the end, nowhere.

A third character kept appearing, face vague, but voice bold. "That's Rona Barrett over there," the figure pointed. "Fucked her way to the top!"

I couldn't let that happen. I had to be able to climb to the top, without Steve, without anybody's help really.

But I had to keep working for Steve, too. Why shouldn't I? He'd shown me affection. Could I help it that he and Eydie were the perfect duo?'

It wasn't easy. It was the hardest thing I had had to do in a long time. And it got harder as each day passed.

I watched him slip further from my grasp into hers. For the first time in months, I became depressed. My parents began asking what was wrong. I'd snap, "Nothing! Leave me alone!"

My father knew what it was. "How come Steve isn't calling as much, Rona?" he asked gently. It had been almost a month now since Steve had come to our house for dinner. And that time he had had to leave early.

Then came my sixteenth birthday party. I'd invited about one-hundred people. Before they came, I prayed to God—one final time. At least I told God it would be one final time if only He'd make this last picture right in my head. And then make it come true. "Dear God," I pleaded, "make Steve love me. I love him so much. I'm going to die if you don't. I love him, do you understand? Make him love me. Make him think I'm beautiful. Make him think I'm more beautiful than Eydie. Do me this one favor and I'll never ask for anything again. I promise. I want Steve. I need him. He needs me. I promise."

Steve brought Eydie to the party. I hadn't invited her. It hurt. Still, I hoped. When the cake was carried in, I closed my eyes and wished—wished it all to God again. I pleaded with Him one more time, thinking it so strong that I was afraid they'd all actually hear my thoughts. Then I opened my eyes at last, took the deepest breath I ever had and blew out the candles.

All but one.

"HAAAAAAAPPY BIRRRRRRTHDAAAAAY!"

Everyone filed by and kissed me. Steve was the last. He reached down and, as always, pressed his lips gently onto mine. My body tingled from head to toe. Had God heard? Was this *it?*

"Happy Birthday, sweetheart," he whispered. He followed it with a firm hug. It lasted a second longer than I expected. And when he said the word "sweetheart," there seemed something extra in it.

But it must have been the birthday punch. For a few months later, I found out that Steve had asked Eydie to marry him. I didn't find it out from Steve.

I read it in Walter Winchell's column.

I wanted to kill myself.

That was new to me. I'd wanted to die a thousand, five thousand times in my life. I'd never thought of actually killing myself until now.

From the first moment I'd heard him sing, I'd known he was special.

I'd worked for him like no one had ever worked. No fifteen-year-old, anyway. During Easter vacation, I had spent almost every waking hour taking his records around to the radio stations. "You're going to drive me nuts till I listen to these, aren't you?" Deejay Brad Phillips shrieked at me the eighth time I got into his office. While in the waiting room, I'd written a dozen letters saying:

"Join The Steve Lawrence Fan Club And Get Five Autographed Photos, A Pin, Membership Card And—"

Hundreds, literally hundreds of responses each day had poured into the office for months, some with dozens of names of potential new members, members who could attend our once-a-month meetings, possibly attend our three-day convention where we'd figure out still more ways to promote Steve in the coming years.

He'd taken me to dinner at his parents' house.

He'd appreciated me.

He'd kissed me.

He was marrying someone else.

I wanted to kill myself.

I even thought about how to do it. But I could never get the picture perfect in my mind. Still, there were moments when I felt I had to end my life. In a way, this was the worst setback I'd ever suffered. It was true that at sixteen I'd done more and learned more of the world outside than probably all my classmates put together. Yet everything I'd done, all I'd learned, *was through what I'd been able to do for someone else*. If that someone else kept leaving, what future was there for me?

But I couldn't get the picture right. Of Rona Barrett dead. Something inside me that I couldn't put my finger on just wouldn't let me do it. If I had to say what it was, the closest I could come would be a thought that still kept popping into my head even when I was the most absolutely depressed. *There must be something better. How could I have gone through all that only to have it end like this?*

I quit working for Steve Lawrence and threw myself into my schoolwork.

CHAPTER FIVE

As the years rolled on, I often found myself returning to my private dream world where I could think more clearly about my road map to Mt. Somewhere. I knew it was out there and I was determined to get there.

I often wondered, as I sat facing my dressing-table mirror, why the hell it took so long for the years to come and go. "Nothing's simple," I would hear myself saying. "Nothing!" It frustrated me beyond understanding that the things I wanted did not happen when I wanted them to happen—right then and there! Now.

Nothing in my life was yielding rewards. I graduated high school as salutatorian that December of my fifteenth year. I should have been valedictorian. I'd worked for it, damn it! I deserved it. Nobody else could come near me, but then in September of that year Regina Boyle transferred into the school, and by November I got the news that Regina's grade point average was two-tenths of a point higher than mine. Caught between screaming and crying in my class advisor's office, I controlled my emotions just enough to point out that Regina hadn't been in the school a year and it wasn't fair.

My advisor was sympathetic, maybe even a little guilty, but she was firm. "I'm sorry, Rona, but they changed the rule this semester. As long as Regina's been here for the complete term there's nothing we can do about it."

So that was that. I was salutatorian of the senior graduating class, but as far as I was concerned, if I didn't come out on top I might as well have been on the bottom—like the class dummy!

I entered N.Y.U. much to my reluctance. I had desperately wanted to go to an out-of-town college—especially Cornell University, where I had gotten a partial scholarship to study medicine, one of the three careers I was contemplating. But my parents thought I was much too young to be away from home. Again, they won. But I won, too. N.Y.U. was bloody expensive. I knew my father would have preferred my entering a city college, but having me still within his grasp meant so much to him, he'd pay anything for that privilege. I took advantage of it. It was my only small consolation, but in the end it really didn't assuage my feelings. I really had very little in common with most of the students I met. The girls, it seemed, were more interested in getting MRS degrees than an education. And the fellows were hoping their "education" would keep them out of the service or give them another four years of "freedom" until it was necessary to go into daddy's successful clothing business or law practice or brokerage house.

So I enrolled as a pre-med student at Washington Square. I had it in my head that only I could discover the cause of my affliction, and becoming the most important medical researcher in the world would eventually enable me to do it. But it only took me one semester to realize I could never spend ten years trying to become a doctor at that school. If I did, I was bound to graduate as a "lunatic-of-medicine" prepared only for an internship at Bellevue's crazy ward. The following semester I switched to pre-law. I was equally convinced that what the world really needed was a dedicated attorney who could right the wrongs of the oppressed. I dreamed of becoming the greatest female attorney of our time. Unfortunately, my mother's brother, my Uncle Jack, whom I adored, was a prominent attorney and adamant beyond legal description about lady legal-eagles. He threatened to make sure I would never pass the New York bar, and I decided not to fight him. But secretly I never believed a word he said. Eight years of law school was also too long at N.Y.U. As I entered my sophomore year, I decided to take the advice of my Uncle Joe. He was my father's brother and the only member of our entire family, on both sides, who believed in me. My third career choice was actually my first—I wanted to go into some phase of show business. I had been showbiz-bit by my early days with Eddie Fisher. But since my parents were so convinced anyone who was involved in show business had to be a degenerate, I really couldn't find it within myself to make matters worse at home by suggesting that I become a permanent member of that society. However, with my uncle standing beside me, giving me courage and confidence, I switched schools and entered N.Y.U.'s School of Commerce, majoring in communicative arts. Much to my surprise, my father did not bat an eyelash. He was still thrilled that I was at home and getting an education.

Despite my making the dean's list, getting an education no longer had the same meaning for me as it had in the past. I had tasted the outside world, and I liked its bittersweet flavor. I wanted more. My few friends at school didn't understand that. Not one of them had been on the outside yet, having all been carefully insulated by their parents. My thinking was so different from theirs and I had so little in common with them, I was soon a total outsider looking in. This only added to my unhappiness. I was again alone, feeling like a misfit. My greatest mistake was to mention that I knew and had worked for Eddie Fisher and Steve Lawrence. I was again the class freak. Only this time it was for another reason. I never even got pledged to a sorority. With only a half-dozen credits to go to obtain my B.S. degree, I left school. My father never forgave me. I only regretted not having gone to law school.

I even quit my job at Asher & Brown, a public relations firm which handled a lot of Steve Lawrences. The job just didn't mean that much to me now. I'd started at the top with Eddie and Steve, and handling a lot of other singers was just like making carbon copies of an original and that just wasn't quite good enough.

I didn't have too much success with boys either. Somehow after Steve, nothing mattered much. I rarely dated except for one boy I had met at college. He was a lawyer-to-be. And my parents adored him. He was also Jewish and rich. And on top of that, he boasted of being a great lover. After our fourth or fifth date I told him that for a great lover he was a lousy kisser. He laughed. We became like brother and sister after that. And every boy I met from then on bored me to paralysis. What it boiled down to was that I was slowly, subconsciously substituting my feelings about males for my feelings about a career in show business, which just had to be better. After all, I would be with *stars*. And *stars* had to be better than other people. And maybe one day I'd be a *star* too. And then I would be different. Then no one would ever mishandle me again.

Because of that, I never really left my other life completely. I saw movies just as much as ever, went to the openings of all the important plays. One night I saw an old pal, Fay, at the opening of *Dark at the Top of the Stairs* We had a cup of coffee afterwards.

"You're lucky Steve married Eydie, " she said. "He's a Mama's boy at heart. You need a real man."

"Where is he?" I joked. "I've got men like Kate Smith's got slenderness. " But I added, "If I had the right job, it would be O.K."

"Hey!" she said. "Could be I can help."

Fay knew of this editor, Bessie Little, one of the top fan magazine editors, who needed a gal Friday. Bessie ran the women's magazine division of Magazine Management, Inc.

Fay made an appointment for me the following day. I figured I'd start as a secretary, gradually go from assistant editor to Bessie's right arm. If *I* couldn't do it, who could?

"Let's get something straight between us," Bessie Little said before she even said hello. "If you think this job is going to lead you to an editorship of one of our magazines, think again, girlie. I used to train each of my secretaries to become editors, but no more. No way. It's much harder to find good secretaries than editors, that's why. So if you want to be a gal Friday, fine and good. Yes, you'll be overly qualified for the job, you'll be brighter than some of my editors right now who have been working here for years. But that's the way it's going to be. Do you want it, girlie? If you want it, take it! But it's typing, filing, billing, secretarial duties. It's nothing more!"

We both thought about it for the weekend. On late Monday afternoon Bessie called. If I wanted the job I could have it.

I took it!

I was right. Bessie Little may have talked like Katharine

Hepburn or Lauren Bacall and dressed in high-platformed, open-toed, Joan Crawford "fuck-me shoes," but she was as soft underneath as a baby panda. Three weeks after I began working as her secretary, I was editing confession scripts, writing captions for picture stories, working with her editors.

I loved it. I had found a new life. One day I even found myself reading a true confession story—we put out those magazines, too—where a girl was contemplating suicide just because her lover jilted her. I found myself thinking: *Why in the world would she want to do that? She has so much to live for!*

The more stories I read the more I found myself forgetting my own problems. Maybe my life wasn't so bad after all? I had a good job and the nicer I was to Bessie the more work Bessie loaded on me. I found the work exhilarating. I was doing something important. Especially when Bessie made me an associate editor of a new fan mag the company was going to put out.

"You have a magnificent future, my darrrrling . . . and a long life. You have suffered much in the past, and you will have a little more suffering to go. But, ahhh . . . in the end . . . the future . . . she is bright. I see your name spoken on the lips of millions. Your face will light up the screen. You shall be world famous and a beautiful young man will soon appear on your horizon to sweep you off your feet." The gypsy lady with her turban and gold rings on every finger bowed graciously, lifted her head and murmured to me, "That'll be two dollars, my darrrrling." She sounded like Zsa Zsa Gabor, but at that moment I couldn't have cared less if she sounded like Margaret Truman, Mamie Eisenhower, or Zazu Pitts. I pulled an old five-dollar bill from my wallet, carefully folded it, and slipped it to the gypsy lady under the table. The gypsy lady smiled; I smiled, too. My heart was beating so fast I thought I was going to drop dead right there in the Russian-style restaurant.

"Well, what did she say? What did she say? . . . Tell us," Mimi and Sandra asked.

"She's been terrific for us," said Mimi, who was my boss at *True Time Confessions*.

I felt shy. I had never been to a palm reader before—or, for that matter, had I ever met anyone who could see into the future. The whole experience at the restaurant had been a trip which I hoped would never end.

"Let's go!" I hastily responded. "I'll tell you in the taxi back to the office."

We quickly paid our check and left and found a cab in front just getting rid of a passenger.

Squeezed between the two women, I couldn't decide which one to direct my conversation to, so I looked straight ahead at the back of the driver's neck and spoke to it. "She told me I'd be famous and that I'm going to meet a guy who's going to sweep me off my feet."

"Famous!" exclaimed Mimi. "Doing what?"

"Well, she didn't actually say."

"Well, why didn't you ask her?"

"Well, I didn't think about it. After all, I'd never been to one of those fortune tellers before. I didn't know how it worked. . . . What are you supposed to do? Ask questions?"

"Of course, dummy!" Sandra answered, as if she were fed up with my naivete. "How in the hell do you find out anything unless you ask questions!"

"Well, one thing's for sure. You'll make a lousy reporter so don't ever become one!" Mimi smirked, lighting a cigarette which she forced into her long, fancy holder.

I thought she looked ridiculous smoking a cigarette in a holder. Mimi was just not the holder type. She weighed two-hundred and fifty pounds dripping wet; her hair was always disheveled, and her fingers were so fat I wondered how she kept from making typing mistakes on her manuscripts. But she had a quick wit and an extremely bright mind and this compensated a great deal for all of her other problems. I liked Mimi a lot—especially her intelligence factors.

But Mimi had no fondness for me. She seemed almost to hate me, which I couldn't fathom for anything. It hurt me deeply. From the moment I met Mimi, I felt I knew her even though I didn't know her. Fat people always have a way of knowing each other—or so I thought. Though I weighed nothing like Mimi, I could feel her same frustrations. I knew something horrible must have occurred in her life to make her hide behind layers of fat. It had to be her great protection against some awful hurt. Maybe she'd never find the answer. I only felt Mimi needed an understanding friend and I was willing to be it. Mimi, on the other hand, made it very clear to me that no matter what, *she* wasn't going to be it. Mimi viewed me as a threat. I was the youngest associate editor to ever work at Magazine Management, Inc.—one of the largest pulp publishing houses in America.

One day Mimi, in all her two-hundred-and-fifty-pound glory, clumped through the office, placed her large hands flat on my desk and exclaimed so the whole place could hear, "Who the hell do you think you are?" Her words were spit through clenched teeth. "I've been here ten years and in a few months you've taken over—or so you think! Listen here, Miss Illiterate! I run the women's division of Magazine Management for Bessie Little . . . NOT YOU! If there are any editorial changes to be made, I WILL MAKE THEM! . . . NOT YOU! . . . You're just a punk around here. A crazy one at that! All of us know you're crazy. Even our psychiatrist says you're crazy . . . and pushy . . . and God knows what else! So let me set you straight. Stop buttering up the boss. You've gone as far as you're going in this organization—if I can help it! And my ten years here WILL help it! Stop taking over! That's an ORDER! You want something . . . ASK ME! Don't go directly to Bessie. You hear?"

I heard her all right. But I couldn't believe what I was hearing. I hadn't done anything wrong. I knew it. Everything Bessie had asked me to do I'd done—even working overtime to help get the brown-line to the printer. What did Mimi mean? I hadn't taken Mimi's job away. And why did she call me illiterate? I was so choked up I found myself speechless with tears streaming down my cheeks while eighteen girl editors, assistant editors, copy writers, readers, etc. swiveled in their chairs, staring in my direction, gaping like mentally retarded adults I had seen depicted in *The Snake Pit*. I would never forget their expressions. Some of the girls had half-smirks on their lips. Each in their own way seemed to enjoy what was happening, like their souls had been hungering for a good war for months.

I gave them what they wanted. I glared right back into Mimi's eyes, pulling every inch of my five-foot-one-inch body up straight, and screamed, "Mimi, I'm not the one who is crazy! YOU ARE! No wonder you see your psychiatrist five days a week. You're crazy with jealousy . . . and ENVY . . . because Bessie likes me as much as she likes you. And you've been here ten years and I've become as close to her in a few months as you have in ten years. And for this you blame me—you blabbering idiot! Maybe if you lose some weight around your brain as well as your ass you won't need to see a doctor any more, Mimi! I don't want Bessie. . . . I want to learn something . . . and not YOU or any one of your sick cohorts are going to change that! You get the PICTURE? GET AWAY FROM MY DESK or I'll crack you with this ruler!"

I lifted my sharp-edged ruler and held it tightly in my fist, waving it in front of Mimi. I cracked the ruler across the desk.

Mimi turned on her plump heels and went back to her cubbyhole. Feeling safe behind the partition, she stuck her head out the door once more and yelled across the room.

"I'm BOSS! Don't forget it, Rona!"

"I won't, Mimi, dear," I yelled back—a swagger in my voice so that everyone at Magazine Management just knew who had won the battle.

Twelve years later I was to read of Mimi's death in the Hollywood trade papers. She was forty-two. Death was attributed to natural causes. I suspected that she died of a broken heart after years of loneliness, frustration, and bitterness.

CHAPTER SIX

Have you ever imagined what it would be like living among the beautiful people? The Marquee Stars? The Billboard Headliners? Those big, glamorous, gorgeous people whom Walter Winchell and Dorothy Kilgallen wrote about in their daily columns?

Have you ever wondered what it would be like to be part of their lives? To walk into Downey's Restaurant, which everyone called the poor man's Sardi's because old man Downey's prices weren't as exorbitant as Vincent Sardi's and besides you didn't have to wear a tie or be the biggest star on Broadway to get a good booth and be recognized by all the waiters and half the customers? To have Archie, his youngest son, pull you out of the line that burgeoned up Eighth Avenue and have you placed in a booth everyone knew was reserved for VIP's?

I loved every minute of it. I often wondered why the Downey boys were so extra good to me. I wasn't anybody yet. An associate editor of a big movie magazine, but certainly no Winchell or Kilgallen. Yet they treated me as if I were, and because I felt so loved and wanted and, most of all, so high-holy important, Downey's became *my* place . . . my special spot on earth. The Downeys even bought me a race horse, which they housed for me at Belmont Park and called Lady Rona. And Pop Downey's oldest son, Jimmy, who loved me like another sister, even

got me a rent-controlled apartment in his building right
around the corner from the restaurant. There was only
one hitch: I suddenly had three roommates and the apartment had only one bedroom, a living room the size of
a cracker box, and a pullman kitchen. The bedroom had
one double bed and one single bed and the only way to
get in and out of the room was by climbing over beds.
Forget the closet space. There was none. But when you
live with three struggling actresses you don't have to worry
about things like that. No one had any money for clothes
so there was no real closet problem—until, that is, I arrived
with my Klein's wardrobe, which looked like it had been
bought at Saks or Bonwit's.

My mother loved to shop at Klein's. I hated the place
with a vengeance. Grabbing, pushing, ugly women ready
to scratch your eyes out if by mistake you pull something
they pull at the same time. I hated the fact there were
never any real salesgirls around to help you try on clothes.
But for my mother, Klein's was her place. To eye a dress
originally priced at two hundred dollars and make sure
no one purchased it until the price had been brought down
to twenty dollars gave her a thrill that I later equated
with a fantastic orgasm. So it was no wonder that my
three roomies suddenly thought they had gotten themselves a Miss Rich Bitch in their household.

As it turned out, I was the only regularly employed
member of the foursome. Therefore, I became responsible
for paying the rent on time, the telephone and electric
bill, and buying the food. I was just glad my father was
in the grocery business. Every week he brought us a supply
of food. And every time he visited the cracker box apartment he would get tears in his eyes and say to me: "Darling, why do you need this? Why don't you come home

to your beautiful room? What are you doing to yourself? A nice girl like you doesn't have to live in a dump like this." He'd shake his head, kiss me good-bye, and sadly drive home to Queens.

Answer: Read on.

My mother couldn't figure out for the life of her why a kid like her daughter had to leave a nice home and move in with "three bums." It made no difference to her when I swore on a stack of Bibles that three of us were still virgins!

My roommates were also filled with lofty ambitions. They all dreamed of becoming stars. There was Diane Ladd (no relation to Alan), a dynamite southern package, who was one of the finest young actresses I've ever known. She also was a talented writer. Unfortunately, Diane never really made it. For a brief moment she caught the fancy of Walter Winchell and he began bouqueting her Mondays, Wednesdays, and Fridays. But the bouquets eventually wilted and Diane was left frustrated. She gained momentary recognition again when she married the very talented Bruce Dern, another struggling actor. Their marriage dissolved several years later after the tragedy of their small daughter drowning in their swimming pool.

Madlyn Rhue, whom we affectionately called Mickey, shared another corner. Mickey was basically lazy. Whenever she wanted to work, few producers would turn her down. She had a unique semitic beauty and a unique sincerity. But Mickey was more concerned with being in love and often dropped her career for a man. She eventually married actor Tony Young of the short-lived "Gunslinger" TV series, but when his career took a dive it was difficult for them both to hold on. Tony went to Europe to become a big spaghetti-Western attraction, but he never

became popular with American producers, and eventually
he and Mickey divorced. Mickey was the first of the girls
to leave the apartment. Hollywood was home town and
she thought she'd have a better chance of making it there
after a few years in New York. When I put her in a taxi
for the airport, I didn't think I'd ever see her again, and
I cried as she drove away.

Judy Loomis was my third roommate, an all-American
beauty with the best teeth I'd ever seen until Robert
Redford came along. Judy found greater success modeling
and eventually did very well in TV commercials. I lost
track of Judy after I left for Hollywood, almost a year
after Mickey, but I will always remember her understanding and kindness.

My fourth roomie didn't live in all the time, because
her parents had a pretty terrific place on West End Avenue. But once in a while when she wanted a night away
or just a place to crash, Suzanne Pleshette made our little
apartment home. She was just out of high school and
attending the Neighborhood Playhouse when we met.
Suzy was always a most disciplined and dedicated actress,
and I knew she would be a success—she had it written
all over her face in big capital letters which spelled D-E-
T-E-R-M-I-N-A-T-I-O-N N-O M-A-T-T-E-R W-H-A-T!
From the day Suzy left the Neighborhood Playhouse she
was never out of work.

Through our little apartment paraded starving young
actors like Jimmy Dean, Nick Adams, Mark Damon, Tony
Perkins, and dozens of others, all unknown at the time.
One I would always remember, even if he hadn't become
notorious in later years.

He lived in a trashy section of New York and was dating
Diane. He didn't have a pot to urinate in. He played a

mean piano and was very cute, though, and girls were more than willing to have him use their pots. He was the kind all females like to mother. He liked being mothered. Except afterward, he'd complain that his girlfriends were too possessive!

One night, while fast asleep, I thought I heard the doorbell ring. No one wanted to get out of bed to answer it. It kept ringing. I finally staggered out of bed, tripping over one of the other girls. It was a little past 4:00 A.M. Our door, unfortunately, had no peephole, so I asked, "Who's there?"

"It's me and I'm hungry."

"Who's *me?*"

"Just open up. It's Di's guy."

I opened the door. I was always opening the door.

Just a crack, though. Before I knew it, this huge creature lunged forward, grabbing and screaming like some wild maniac, "I'm gonna rape you! This is it, baby! You're finally gonna lose that fuckin' cherry!" And with that, he grabbed me. I screamed in terror.

Every light and every door in the building seemed to do an instant turn-on, including our own.

"Wha's happening . . . happening?" my roommates screamed.

I was about to pass out. Then I heard Diane say, "Oh, my God. It's only *Warren.*"

Yes, friends.

It was *only* Warren Beatty.

He had come for a free meal.

I should have known anyone making that kind of an entrance would want a bowl of Italian spaghetti, not a Jewish cherry.

Then, I was scared spitless. Now I look upon it differently. I see how virtually everything Warren did was an "act" of some sort or another, just as his "love" for girl after girl was actually more performance than genuine feeling.

No doubt it all would mean deep, dark, fascinating secrets to some expert psychiatrist. To me, it meant two things: (1) Warren was bold and unpredictable mainly because he was a little boy—a little boy who will probably never grow up. Warren Beatty is afraid to find out who and what he is. As his own sister, Shirley MacLaine, said to me about him: "He empathizes—from the waist down only." And (2) Warren Beatty would reach the pinnacle.

There was something about Downey's that made the unconfident feel confident and secure—like a mother's womb. At first I didn't recognize the restaurant as a safe place. I only saw it as my new-found pinnacle of heavenly excitement, glamour, and adventure. . . . A place where rising stars like Tony Franciosa and Shelley Winters drank Irish coffee . . . and a big, black, handsome actor named Sidney Poitier would while away the late hours talking out his dreams of stardom. . . . A place where Paul Newman of the ocean-blue eyes would find solace until his first Broadway play would come along to make him a star . . . and later Joanne Woodward . . . and Elia Kazan . . . and Tennessee Williams . . . and Ben Gazzara. . . . And one-eyed Peter Falk, wearing a Colombo-type trench coat even then, would jauntily walk in waving hi to anyone who'd lift their head as he passed by their table.

Some nights, I thought, if someone dropped a bomb on Downey's the future of Broadway—the future of Hollywood—would collapse in an instant. Obliteration of the theater world . . . an entire profession—POOF!—in a second. But most of all, my thinking was shaded by the minor recognition factor I was enjoying. Especially on those nights when the place would be jammed after an opening night and while everyone waited inside and out to get into Downey's, Archie would always have a place for me at the family table. As he pushed me forward, I never once denied to myself how thrilled I was when I could hear people whisper, "Who's she? . . . Must be someone important." And then as I was being seated in the booth, suddenly to be recognized by Paul . . . or Sidney . . . or Shelley . . . or Ben . . . or even sweet, sad Tony Ray with his mournful Pluto eyes, whom I had discovered doing a daytime serial. And there would be a chorus of "Hi, Rona. . . . How goes it? . . . Come and sit with us when you have a chance."

"Thanks," I'd wave to all of them as if I were Eleanor Roosevelt, my idol, waving to her constituency in deep gratitude. *If this is what having influential friends is all about, I'm going to have all the influential people at my feet someday,* I quietly murmured to my secret self.

It was only months and months later that I began recognizing Downey's as a haven for lonely people, frightened people, insecure people . . . a place where none of these people had to feel shame or hurt for whatever reasons. They all had a common bond. They all knew it. It was their silent language, which they all knew how to speak more eloquently than some of the words they spoke on stage. And I, Rona Barrett, was just the same, except for an extraordinary ambition to reach Mt. Somewhere where it all had to be different. Better. It just had to be. I knew it!

"Why don't you become another Winchell or Hedda Hopper?" Tony Ray blurted out one evening as we dined at Downey's. "The whole world tells you their problems.

You've obviously got shoulders broader than Mr. Atlas's."

"Tony, you're crazy," I answered as I stuffed a large spoonful of linguini and clams into my mouth.

"I'm not! . . . I happen to be very serious. And I've been giving it a lot of thought. You know more about movies and the theater than anyone our age I've ever met. And all the young actors can talk to you. You know about our frustrations. You have them yourself, but somehow you manage to keep yourself intact, while most of us fall apart. Besides, Winchell and Kilgallen and the ladies from Hollywood never write about young, upcoming stars. Their whole world revolves around Clark Gable and Lana Turner and Irene Dunne. And Winchell's bouqueting J. Edgar Hoover every other day when he isn't bouqueting Kate Smith. C'mon, Rona, you've been wondering what in the hell to do with your life. You don't want to edit movie magazines the rest of your days. . . . Think about it. It's a hell of an idea, and you're the only one I know who can pull it off."

While Tony spoke, I continued stuffing myself with linguini and wondering why someone was always trying to get me to do something with my life when all I wanted was to get hooked up with some important guy and be that great woman behind him. Why did everyone think I could be SOMEONE? Sure, I was smart. Sure I got great grades. Sure I made the dean's list in college and sure I had huge shoulders for anyone to cry on. But what was so unique about that? For all the diamonds in South Africa, I couldn't figure it out. The only thing I was beginning to recognize was that the kind of man under whose umbrella I'd like to walk wasn't in my grasp. And it was slowly becoming obvious to me that the only way I could get him was by putting myself on a new plane—in a new sphere—and when an opportunity came I could grasp it. My parents certainly had not given me the life style I yearned for. They were even afraid to send me away to an out-of-town college. Even when I got a scholarship to Cornell University.

And now, sitting across from Tony, whom I worshipped because of his sensitivity and his deep understanding, I wondered why even he couldn't see me for myself. I adored Tony, but we both knew nothing would ever come of it. As we sat across from each other, sharing my nineteenth birthday, he slipped me a present. It was a gold charm in the shape of a typewriter. With it was a note: Rona, darling. Seriously think about what I have just told you. I think you'll make one helluva reporter. The best Hopper and Winchell there ever was. And every time you look at this charm remember these words. I love you. . . . Happy Birthday . . . Tony.

I read the sample column over a thousand times as I sat at my desk waiting for Bessie Little to arrive. I practically knew it by heart. But would Bessie like it? It was different. It was bright and young and fresh and funny. I called the column "Rona Barrett's Young Hollywood," and it was loaded with names—young names, up and coming names: Tony Perkins, Jimmy Dean, Nick Adams, Paul Newman, Harry Guardino, Mark Damon, Tony Ray. . . . They were all there.

Bessie hadn't even taken off her coat when I bounded into her office, exclaiming, "Bessie, I've got to speak to you. I've got a fantastic idea and I want you to have it for *Screen* Stars. Are you ready to listen?"

"Jeeesus, Rona. Can a girl have a cup of coffee first? "

"Oh! What do you want, black or with cream today."

"You know I only drink it black. . . . Boy, you must have had some night last night."

"You can say that again. . . . I'll be back in a jiff. The coffee man's still outside."

Bessie was running a brush through her hair when I returned.

"Well, will you listen now."

"O.K., O.K.! What's on your mind?"

"I now know what I want to do with my life, Bess. I want to be a columnist like Winchell and Hopper." Before Bess could inject a thought of her own, I was spieling. "Someday those guys are going to die and there's no one around that I know of who's going to take their place. So why shouldn't it be me? Besides, I've got a gimmick, a new way of doing it. I don't want to write about the Gables and the Bogarts. They're not part of my era. There's a new era out there, Bess. You can feel it. A young America is on the rise. Their ideas are different. Their tastes are different. Years ago a Marlon Brando couldn't get arrested if he showed up in Hollywood wearing blue jeans and a torn T-shirt. But today it's news. There's a new world out there, and I know those people living in it because I'm one of them. I'm a contemporary of the Brandos and the Newmans and the kids on Broadway, but they don't have a spokesman because they're not big enough yet. Hopper and Parsons won't give them a mention until Jack Warner or Darryl Zanuck puts them under contract, and worse yet, not until they make an A picture. But I will. And I know how they think and how they feel is how other young people who are not in the business feel. I can be their spokesman. I just know it, Bess. I can feel it. . . . Look at the guys in the music business today. Elvis Presley. He's a giant and not even Parsons will talk about him. She thinks he's disgusting because of the way he wiggles. What does she know? Can't you see that?" I was running out of breath. "So you see, I've come up with this idea of writing a column only about *young* stars. I want to call it Rona Barrett's Young Hollywood. Will you let me try it in the magazine?"

Bess sat back in her swivel chair, staring at me in disbelief. She lit a cigarette and the deafening silence sent butterflies to my stomach. Bess leaned forward, "Rona, I've never met a writer yet who didn't want to be a columnist. What makes you think you'll be the successful exception?" Before I could answer Bessie was continuing, "No, Rona. I think the idea stinks. Forget it!"

In disbelief I replied, "You really mean that, don't you? . . . I can't believe it. . . . I can't believe you can't see the logic in what I just told you."

"Well, that's the way it is, Rona. Win a few, lose a few. Now why don't we get back to doing what you're paid to do, huh?"

I walked out of Bessie Little's office, shaking my head. The stars must have been in a cockeyed position that day. It just didn't make sense, but something inside of me told me not to put the idea back into a drawer. It was a good idea. I knew it. I felt it. There had to be someone who'd believe me.

I wondered about Evelyn Paine, the new young editor of *Photoplay,* my company's biggest competitor. The whole publishing world had been shocked when old man Manheimer hired Evelyn as editor of the oldest and most successful magazine in the movie fan field. She was young and gorgeous and had style. She actually looked more like a fashion model or the editor of *Vogue* than the editor of a movie magazine. Neither Manheimer nor any of the

other publishers had ever hired an editor under fifty. Bessie
Little was probably the only exception. She was in her
late thirties when she came to Magazine Management,
Inc. And if she hadn't gained such a super reputation during the war editing a woman's mag that had
a circulation of five million (and she had only been about
twenty-one then) Magazine Management, Inc. would
never have hired her. But Evelyn Paine was no more than
twenty-six—seven years my senior. She just had to think
differently than Bessie. But how could I get to her? It
became my new project.

As fate would have it, one day I was seated at my desk
when a young actor named Bob Evans came to the office
for an interview. Bob had been signed by Twentieth Century-Fox for a part in Hemingway's *The Sun Also Rises*.
Why he wanted to become an actor was still a mystery
to everyone. He was one of Walter Winchell's favorite
darlings, a café society boy who ran an enormous sports-
wear company with his brother, Charles. He was a millionaire several times over and needed to be an actor like
a hole in the head, but he had that burning hunger I
began to see often—the show biz bug had consumed another victim—and almost instantly we seemed to be life-
long friends. After Bob's interview with Mimi, who had
become editor of our new movie magazine, he was on his
way across the street to *Photoplay* to see his good friend
Evelyn Paine.

"You know her?" I sort of asked in a half-whisper,
hoping no one would spot the gleeful anticipation beating
beneath my five-sizes-too-large sweater.

"Very well," Bob whispered. "Need her?"

"Uh-huh!" I nodded, noticing Bob's warm smile and
his perfectly white teeth, emphasized by the suntan he

wore all year long. God, he was smooth and smooth-look-
ing. No wonder all those Seventh Avenue models stood
in line waiting and praying he'd give one of them a tumble.
And no wonder he always got his name in Winchell's
column. He was just one of those types you couldn't ignore
the moment he walked into a room. And the armpieces
he usually brought along clinched it.

"I'll tell her to expect your call."

"Thanks, Bob. If what I have in mind works, I'll never
forget you."

I didn't learn until years later how solidly Bob Evans
had put me over with Evelyn Paine. By then Bob had
given up his acting career to become the production chief
of Twentieth Century-Fox. Bob and I have remained
friends throughout the years, the pattern of our lives
criss-crossing each other's at moments that became "the
crucial hours" of our lives.

My meeting with Evelyn went better than I had antici-
pated and Evelyn offered me the back page of *Photoplay*
to inaugurate the new idea. When Bessie heard about it,
she nearly fainted. I quit Magazine Management, Inc.,
convinced fame and riches were just around the corner.

"By the way, Evelyn, what are you going to pay for
the column?" I asked a few days later. I just knew it
was going to be around $800 a month. That was the going
rate for all top movie columnists like Hopper and Parsons
and Winchell.

"Well, I'll start you off at twenty-five dollars a column."

"TWENTY-FIVE DOLLARS A COLUMN?" I
shrieked. "I can't live on that!"

"Well, Rona, what did you expect? A Parsons' fee at
your stage in the game?"

"Yes, to be honest with you. . . . Why, Evelyn, I just

quit Bess when you offered me the job. What am I going
to do now?"

"I'll tell you what. Why don't you take a trip this
summer to Hollywood? Meet a few stars, give me some
story ideas and maybe between the column and the stories
which I pay $250 for, you can learn to support yourself."

I gulped. How could I have been so naive? I taxied back
to the apartment wondering if I'd ever be able to afford
a taxi again. Was this what fame was all about? Lots
of recognition but no money?

My thoughts raced to Ben Gary. Maybe he could give
me some encouragement. What was it he had told me
a few months before my eighteenth birthday when he read
my astrological chart for the first time? I thought hard.
I hadn't paid much attention to everything Ben had told
me, especially when right off the bat he told me my love
chart had one of the worst astrological afflictions in it
he'd ever seen, and that my chances for ever getting
married were not impossible but doubtful.

Ben Gary was an astrologer. I knew very little about
astrology up until the time I met Ben. I only knew that
astrology had something to do with the stars and the
influences they seemed to have on each human's life,
depending on the hour of their birth, the month, the year,
and the place. What it all really meant I never knew or
cared. But from the moment I met Ben, who was the
best friend of one of my dearest friends, Marvin Paige
(who produced the radio show "Luncheon" at Sardi's),
I began changing my thinking. Marvin had lots of contacts
and he liked me a lot. I was a good companion for him,
especially when he had to go to all the opening nights
on Broadway. How Ben and Marvin met, I never quite
remembered. The stories were never the same so I imag-

ined neither one of them wished for anyone to know the truth about anything, let alone each other.

Ben was by far the ugliest human I had ever encountered—except for myself, at times. He looked like an albino and drank beer for breakfast, lunch, and dinner. But despite his physical peculiarities, Ben Gary was a darling guy—with ethics yet. He thought it was improper to read someone's chart before their eighteenth birthday. I had been in my last year of college when we met, and he promised to do my chart as an eighteenth birthday gift. Up until that time Ben refused to tell me anything, except to ask why my legs looked so perfect when my chart showed they shouldn't be. I wondered if Marvin had said anything to Ben about my physical handicap or whether Ben had even seen me climb the stairs to Marvin's apartment and put two and two together. Each swore on a stack of Bibles, NO!

Ben Gary had decided to give me my birthday present two months early. He knew I had been despondent over my work, and he knew from the chart that I shouldn't be. The chart was never wrong, and Rona Barrett's chart was brilliant. It wasn't going to be easy for me, but one day I'd be famous, rich, successful. My name would become a household word. I might even produce movies and write plays. And who knows, as badly aspected as my fifth house of romance was, maybe someday, later on in life when my karmic debts were met and I had learned the true meaning of love and God as one—who knew? . . . Maybe the aspects would change and the right man would come into my life. Ben Gary was blinded by beer when he read for me that August, right before my eighteenth birthday.

The only thing I was interested in learning was when

I was going to get married, what kind of man would he be, where would I meet him . . . and oh yes, what about my career?

Ben, obviously had chosen a poorly aspected day, despite his diligence in looking daily, if not minute by minute, in his ephemeris. From the instant he told me my love life was for naught, I blocked out most of what he had to say about my work and my career. I only heard bits and pieces. . . . Success, yes . . . writing, yes . . . producing, yes . . . books (he's crazy) . . . but no marriage. God must be punishing me, I thought as Ben read the chart. I thought he also had said something about better luck in another part of the country. I tried to remember. Was it California?

I dialed his number. The line was busy. It was always busy. I dialed it again. I listened to the busy signals. I kept the phone to my ear and wondered what Tony Ray was doing. I wondered if Steve was happy with Eydie. Eddie had married his first gentile, Hollywood's sweetheart, Debbie Reynolds. The country had dubbed them America's Sweethearts. They were the 1950's answer to Mary Pickford and Douglas Fairbanks. Life just seemed fantastic for everybody, but me. I started to cry, talking to myself as I pressed the receiver closer to my ear, "God! What is it that you want? Won't you tell me! Where do you want me to go? What do you want me to be? I don't know. Help me! Help me! . . . Help me!" I hung up the phone, waited a few minutes, picked it up again, and dialed Ben Gary's number. It was no longer busy.

Ben answered, "Helloooooow." It was him all right. No one ever answered a phone as spooky-like as Ben Gary did. You almost felt as if you were talking to Mr. Inner Sanctum.

"It's me. Rona. I need you, Ben."

"Rooona, darrrrling. What can I do for yooooou?"

"Ben, remember when you read my chart for the first time? You said something about my luck would change if I moved west. Isn't that what you said?"

"Yeees, that's what I said. You are very well aspected for the West Coast. You will find greater harmony living there and especially getting away from your family. You will find that from the moment you arrive you will feel you have lived in California all your life. . . . I think in another lifetime you were probably some Spanish Princess and you owned TONNNNS of acreage."

I was laughing. Ben Gary always had a way of making me laugh. I wasn't sure if it was due to what he said or how he said it, but suddenly the heavy vise which had kept me in a state of depression all day was no longer there.

My mind was made up. California here comes Rona Barrett.

"Good-bye, sweet Ben Gary. Parting is such sweet sorrow. But on the morrow I leave for Hollywood. Thank you and God bless you . . . and may your chart *not* be wrong, or so help me, Ben, I'll deprive you of your beer the rest of your life!"

CHAPTER SEVEN

Everything seemed to be falling into place. *Photoplay* was giving me the opportunity to write feature articles for them, Ben Gary told me I was well aspected for Hollywood, and on New Year's Eve, 1958, I received a long-distance telephone call from a struggling actor named Michael Landon and his then wife Dodie, inviting me to move into their sumptuous home that had once belonged to Clara Bow.

For sixty dollars a month I could live like a star with a star. I accepted the offer.

My first nine months with the Landons could be a book in itself. Suffice it to say it was one of the best periods of my life, although I wound up supporting all of us on my little articles for which I got paid twenty-five, forty and later on one hundred dollars. When Mike got a job, he always paid me back.

Dodie became my best friend. She was a kook, who kept awful house. How could she help it? We had nine cats pissing everywhere and I think three dogs doing their number. She did have one good trait. She was a great cook and gave great dinner parties, and slowly I began to meet all of Young Hollywood. Dodie even managed to get *me* a date to the Oscars with one of Hollywood's rising stars, Ben Cooper. You do remember Ben? I don't know how she managed it, but I later found out she told Ben I was the editor of *Photoplay*. Poor Ben.

Anyway, nine months later, when I found Mike's attentions toward me appeared not so brotherly, I moved out.

I no longer felt I owed the Landons a perennial live-in. Mike in that first year had gotten himself a series called Bonanza. He thought it would last less than thirteen weeks. So did I. But I thought he was terrific and despite its sure demise would go on to do bigger and better things.

It was July 31, 1959 and Los Angeles looked so clear and perfect I thought for a moment I was walking through some film set at Twentieth Century-Fox. Every peak on every hill of the Hollywood skyline jutted toward the heaven in such clear definition I wondered if perhaps the day weren't some secret special high holy holiday where the mountains offered thanks to the heavens for the glorious green coats bestowed on them. It seemed so unreal, so Hollywood, so like the movies.

I hugged myself.

I thought I was going to burst with happiness. I hadn't remembered being so happy in God only knew how many years. It was a rare feeling; the happy days were so infrequent that when they came there was no way to ignore them. The first year of psychology at N.Y.U. had convinced me I was a classic manic depressive. For years, not being able to understand the highs and the lows of moods which descended upon me in flashes, like one moment to the next, made me so fearful I thought I was going crazy! But how could I be crazy? No one in my family had been mentally ill and mental illness, I thought I had read somewhere, was an inherited genetic factor. That tidbit of unproven knowledge assuaged my fears many times.

I had a lot to look forward to that late afternoon. Marvin Paige, my New York pal, had moved to California a year earlier and was taking me to a swinging Hollywood party. I wondered all day what I would wear. I stared at myself in the bathroom mirror and was glad, once again, that the mirror did not extend all the way to the floor.

God, I was still fat. And God, there was still that bump on my nose. And oh, God! Would I have fat cheeks for the rest of my life? I pinched them hard, hoping to make them disappear. Hoping was about the only thing that kept me going sometimes.

But that Sunday afternoon was different. There was no feeling of apprehension—anywhere. I didn't even seem to mind that I had just undertaken my first enormous step toward responsibility: renting my first apartment . . . all for myself . . . to share with no one. It didn't bother me that I wasn't too sure where I'd get the money to pay the second month's rent, having paid the first and the last to the landlord and the rest of the bank account going to Akron for their choicest weave of woven cotton carpeting which would blanket the barren floors.

Sometimes I wished I had the nerve to kick myself in the ass. Sane people would have rented a furnished flat and not worried about how they were going to buy furniture—little things like a bed to sleep on, some sheets, blankets, dishes, silverware. But not Rona Barrett. When it came to myself it was almost imperative that I make things extra difficult—like some special lesson I had to teach myself or learn or it wasn't going to be good. Deep inside something was always saying that for me it had to be different; if I didn't plant my roots deep, I might find myself running away. My father once accused me

of being a "quitter" when I had lost a job after one week.
I never understood why he said that to me. I had never
quit anything in my life and I hadn't quit the job. I had
been fired for making a typing error—just one—one stink-
ing error after typing twenty-five perfect pages of a pre-
sentation which this advertising company was making to
some big prospective client. But he had called me a quitter!
Maybe what he had really meant to say was that I didn't
have the guts to stand up to my boss and tell him that
everyone is entitled to make one mistake. However, at
the time I dismissed the thought. Secretly I had been glad
I was fired. I felt the position wasn't something that would
ever get me to Mt. Somewhere where I could become Miss
Somebody. And God, being a Somebody sometimes was
even more important than being Mrs. Somebody! Never-
theless, Harry Burstein's words bore deep. And so now,
here I was with an apartment I just couldn't walk away
from if things got too tough. And it was important that
I *not* leave Hollywood. Ben Gary had told me over and
over again before I left New York that fame and fortune
and enormous success would be mine on the West Coast.
I believed him. He had never been wrong before; but more
important, I wanted to believe. If I didn't believe, what
else would be left except to die? And I didn't want to
die—just then. Not that day especially. After all, what
would anyone write on my tombstone? Here lies Rona
Barrett. Nobody! Born October 8th, 1936. Died today. It
was an ugly thought.

My first apartment was above the Sunset Strip. The
building had a quiet elegance. Its small courtyard was
kept clean with seasonal flowers and perfectly trimmed
hedges. The apartment contained one large bedroom, one
medium-sized bathroom, a kitchen, a formal dining room

(which made me feel gracious living was just around the corner) and a living room that was larger than most apartment living rooms I had seen. Besides, it had a huge bay window facing the courtyard.

Oh, yes. How happy I was this day looking around my place, even with its meek possessions: a borrowed bed and an orange crate I used for a desk upon which sat the old Olympia typewriter I had bought with my own earned money. I asked my father if he would buy me one, and like most things I asked him for, he answered, "What d' ya need it for? Gonna be a big letter writer someday?" So I saved my money and bought one on my own. It was on sale at Macy's.

I chuckled realizing how the real estate agent who had found me the apartment had convinced the landlady, Mrs. Wicker, that I was a refined young working woman whom she would be proud to have as a tenant.

"A substantial member of our working community, Mrs. Wicker," she said.

You bet your bottom dollar Mrs. Wicker, I mused as I dug in my purse for my bank book. *You bet I'm substantial . . . Now let's see . . . how much do I have? . . . Why, Mrs. Wicker, you darlin' devil. Rona Barrett has nineteen dollars and twenty-seven cents in her bank account. Substantial, you ask? . . . Thank God you didn't ask to see the passbook!* I threw the little blue book into the top drawer of the Victorian dresser I had bought at a secondhand shop for twelve dollars and repainted white.

Marvin headed his little sports car, which he could ill afford, east on Sunset. He was taking me to astrologer Carroll Righter's home, which was slightly east and slightly north of the Sunset Strip. Carroll was having one of his monthly astrological do's. A Leo Party. After all, it was the end of July, heading into August, and as every astrological buff knows, that period of the year comes under the sign of Leo the Lion.

For some reason, newcomers to Hollywood always find themselves at one of Righter's monthly soirees. This was to be my initiation, though I had been in Hollywood almost a year now.

When we walked through Righter's front door, Marvin who was a Leo, and thus invited to the party, introduced me to my host.

Expecting the usual salutation of "Hello, I'm Carroll Righter. How are you?" I was greeted instead by, "Hello, when's your birthday? No year necessary. Just the month and the date."

Mechanically, I responded, "October 8th. I'm Libra."

"How do you do, Miss Libra. Welcome. Please come in and have some fun. By the way, this should be a big year of change for you."

I looked at Marvin. "So what else is new?"

We both laughed. But somehow that old, grey-haired fox with his cherubic face never forgot who you were. One day, ten years later, Righter would see me at the famed Brown Derby on Vine Street and say, "How nice to see you again, Miss Libra."

The party was in full swing and I found my eyes darting in every direction trying to spot anyone famous. I needed lots of news to fill the three monthly columns I was writing, and my brain never let me forget it. I almost pulled Marvin's arm from his socket when I spied Glenn Ford holding court in a corner of the room, surrounded by ten unrecognizable bodies. I soon discovered the *bods* belonged to aspiring actors who one day hoped to lose their anonymity.

I also spotted my press-agent friend Jack Martin. Jack handled practically every *talented* aspiring actor. Jack had a special ability to recognize those who had it—and those who didn't. Mike Landon had been one of Jack's clients.

Jack and I had met in Downey's the year before I came to Hollywood. Handsome Jody McCrea, Joel's son, had asked Jack to call me when he came to New York. We hit it off immediately. Years later, after Jack had become "My Man Martin in London," he admitted he was scared to death about my coming to Hollywood—thought I was too nice a girl to make it in that vicious town.

In a matter of minutes, Marvin and Jack were passing the word around about me.

"She's the new Hopper and Winchell in town. . . . Writes for three of the biggest movie magazines. . . . Has a lotta muscle. . . . Big time, here. . . . Knows all the big people. . . . Has lotsa money behind her. . . . If you're smart," and suddenly Marvin and Jack would lower their voices as if they were about to spill the biggest, juiciest secret, "you should get close to her. If anybody can help you with your career, Rona Barrett can."

Jack Martin was simply terrific at using the Hitler tactic—as he called it. His philosophy was: If you keep telling someone something about someone long enough, they'll begin to believe it. And suddenly when that person's name is dropped somewhere else, the other person finds himself saying, "Why, Rona Barrett. She's the new Hopper-Winchell in town. Important new lady. Big power."

I was slightly embarrassed by the exaggeration of my position, but I didn't object too strongly. Secretly I wished it were already true. And who knew? Maybe one day soon, their little lie wouldn't be a lie after all.

Anyway, as my eyes darted here and there around Righter's salon I was also quietly blessing Hollywood and its facade. It was obvious no one cared to probe deeply. It seemed it would make little difference to anyone that I didn't have a dime in the bank, that I was probably as broke as they were, that I really didn't know a bloody soul on the Hollywood scene except for a few New York chums like Marvin and Jack.

I was doing my daydream number when suddenly I realized I had been staring at a young man seated in a corner. He looked like a tall string bean. He had a blond bang that constantly kept falling over one of his very blue eyes. He was very attractive, until he stood up, and then I got a totally different impression. He was still big, all right, but his head seemed too small for his body, and he looked like a misfit. Clinging to his arm, devouring every word he had to say, was a *zoftig* towhead. I was fascinated by her enormous, saucer-blue eyes and, from a side view, her somewhat thick, prominent nose. She was rather unattractive in profile, but I liked her smile. She had very straight, even white teeth that sparkled like a toothpaste ad.

The big blue-eyed blonde, noticing me staring, waved me over to where they were standing. "Hi," she said, extending her hand to me, drawing me closer to her and the string bean. I, however, didn't need Carroll Righter to tell me he was star material. It was written all over his face. He had that little-boy-lost appeal and I just knew little and big girls would go ga-ga over him. She, on the other hand, had no ambition to become anything except Mrs. Star. She was from the Quaker country, but it didn't prevent her from smoking and drinking up a storm. She appeared to be extremely easy-going, but when her temper did finally unleash itself, she became as vicious as a fire-spitting dragon. It took me only a few short weeks to realize that the two of them should have been nominated "Most Unlikely Couple To Live Together in a Tiny Apartment." The only thing they had in common was a sick enjoyment of beating each other up. They were classic sado-masochists who found the infliction of pain nothing more than fun-and-game times.

I could not find one intelligent reason for the three of us to have become friends. But somehow we did. I reasoned that the friendship was based on my own morbid curiosity about how two people who claimed to love each other could enjoy beating each other up. It was a new experience for me. And being a journalist with an extremely inquisitive mind, this had to be my introduction to mind-blowing! One night my wish came true.

I was minding my own business and getting ready for bed when the phone rang. It was Sandra.

"He's going to kill me!" she screamed into the phone. "Can I come and hide at your house? He'll never suspect I've gone to you. You're a columnist. He wouldn't dare think of hurting me at your place!"

There was such a pleading, urgent sound in her voice, I found myself saying, "Gee, Sandra, I don't mind. But I just moved into this apartment. I don't have a stick of furniture, except for a small bed. And furthermore, I promised my landlady that I was a terrific tenant and hardly knew a soul."

"Honestly, I don't care if I have to sleep on the floor. Please. Just help me."

"O.K.! O.K.!"

The phone clicked off and in a few minutes there was a knock on my door. It sounded frantic. Sandra looked

ready for the morgue. Several bruises stood out starkly
on her arms and face. She didn't have a stick of makeup
on and her mouth was so swollen it looked like it had
been used as a punching bag.

"My God!" I exclaimed. "What in the world happened
to you?"

"He's crazy! He's crazy!" It was the only response she
could make.

"Well, obviously he *is* crazy . . . but for God's sake
why in the hell do you continue living with him?"

"Because I love him!"

"Oh, bullshit, Sandra! Don't give me that line anymore.
I wasn't born yesterday—despite what you all think."

Grabbing hold of my shoulders for what appeared to
be physical and moral support, she cried, "But I swear
. . . this is the end. I'm moving out. I'm never going to
see him again. I hate him—the son of a bitch! . . . By
the way, don't answer the phone if it should ring. He just
may try to call here."

"But I thought you said he didn't know you were coming
here!"

"Well, I don't think . . . but you never know with him."

The phone rang. I looked at Sandra.

"Promise me!" There was such frantic pleading in her
voice.

"But I can't let the phone just keep on ringing. It sounds
like the place is coming apart. With no furniture it's like
an echo chamber in here."

But the ringing didn't stop. I looked at my kitchen clock.
It was two in the morning.

"Holy mackerel! If I don't answer that phone, Sandra,
my landlady's going to kill me!"

But suddenly the phone stopped ringing.

We looked at each other. Sandra was completely exhausted. I was a nervous wreck. I made a bed for Sandra out of an old quilt my mother had sent me for a housewarming present. We climbed into our respective mattresses, but neither of us could fall asleep. I kept looking over at the illuminated dial on the clock. It was now 3:15. I wished I owned some sleeping pills—anything so I could drown my thoughts. Why had I allowed Sandra to come over? I needed this whole night like a bleeding ulcer. I was finally dozing off when suddenly there was a loud bang at the front door. It startled me so, I nearly fell out of bed. And since Sandra was already sleeping on the floor, she didn't have far to go. She looked like an etching in fright, ghostly white.

"It's him. . . . It's him! . . . Don't let him in," she demanded in a high whisper. "Pretend you're not here."

I tried to pretend. But it was useless. The banging got louder . . . and louder . . . and then there was this voice shouting awful obscenities. "Listen, you *whores!* Get up! I know you're in there!"

"Oh, my God, Sandra! My landlady is going to kick me out! I told her I was a nice girl and very quiet . . . and didn't know a soul." I was peeking through my bedroom window, which faced the front courtyard. A light went on in my landlady's apartment. "I've got to let him in and calm him down, Sandra . . . or we'll both be out on the street!"

But it was too late. The cheap apartment door lock had given way and he was standing in the doorway looking like a raving maniac by the time I reached the living room. I had never seen such a look on anyone's face in my entire lifetime. Was this what mad people, who were locked away in Bellevue Hospital, really looked like?

I cried out, "Oh, my GOD!" Sandra was now by my side.

"I'm gonna *kill* you . . . you cunt!" he hissed, lunging for Sandra. Sandra screamed. He grabbed her by the hair and began whacking her around. Her screams grew louder . . . louder.

"Call the police!" she finally managed to gurgle. I ran for the phone, but he was too quick for me. He stopped pummeling Sandra and tackled me. I fell to the floor. He made another plunge at Sandra as she tried to beat him to the doorway for an exit. Both of us girls were now down on the floor, but at opposite ends of the room.

He didn't know which one to keep his eye on, but it was Sandra he was interested in and not me. Seizing the opportunity, I tried to get up and race to the bedroom where there was another phone, but again he was too quick for me. In a matter of seconds he had not only torn Sandra's nightgown from her body, but he had her head in a hammerlock and was dragging her bodily across the living room to where I was unsuccessfully trying to get to my feet. He whacked me from behind in the bend in my knees, sending me immediately sprawling back to the floor. Not willing to take any more chances, he pulled both phone cords from the wall and yelled to me, "Just lie there, you fat, ugly pig . . . or I'll kill you!"

There was now left no doubt whatsoever in my mind that he was a maniac and capable of doing any-thing—including committing murder!

I believed it was only a matter of minutes before he would kill one of us.

Sandra made a last ditch effort to free herself, but it was no use. The more she struggled, the more vicious he became. He was choking her unmercifully and I could see the blood beginning to leave Sandra's face.

"Stop it! . . . Stop it!" I had managed to get to my feet and was standing over him, trying to pull him off the girl. But my pleas went unnoticed. He was too busy trying to murder the one he said he loved.

I fled to the kitchen. There was still one phone left in the apartment and I hoped maybe it was still working. I picked up the phone and, shaking like a leaf, dialed "O" . . . but there was no sound. I dialed again, this time screaming into the phone, hoping for a miracle or miracles that there would be someone at the other end listening anyway. "Hello! . . . Hello! . . . Help! . . . Somebody! . . . Help!" I cried into the mouthpiece.

But the deafening silence only made the thundering banging I heard going on inside the living room more hideous. It sounded as if someone's head were being bashed against the wall.

I raced back into the living room. I didn't care what happened any more. If I was going to die that night, then I would die, but I wouldn't die without putting up one helluva fight.

"Stop it!" I yelled at him, grabbing a shock of his long blonde hair. "I'll kill you . . . you son-of-a-bitch! . . . Stop it! You're killing that girl! . . . Do you hear me? . . ."

But he just ignored me. He just kept slamming Sandra's head against the wall. And then there was a gush of blood. It splattered all over the place.

"Oh, my God . . . you've killed her! . . . You've killed her!"

The blood poured in every direction. Over the walls. Onto the brand new beige carpet. Onto Sandra. Onto him. Onto me. Everywhere.

I felt myself passing out. And as I fell to the floor I

thought I saw him swing Sandra over his shoulder. Sandra looked dead. She was stark raving nude. He was stark raving mad—a caveman gone berserk.

As blackness overtook me, my last awareness was hearing the ignition on his Maserati turn over and the car roar away into the dawn.

The initiation was over. This was Hollywood. And I had just been paid a visit by two of its up-and-coming citizens: Tarzan and Jane.

I slept on the floor all night and awoke to another bright, sunny California morning, seeming all the more artificial for the patches of drying blood on the walls and carpet. I commanded my aching muscles into obedience and headed for the shower first. Washed, cleaned, and repaired (at least on the surface), I set about trying to clean the place up, and two hours into scrubbing the carpet, my doorbell rang in that polite but authoritative manner landladies use to announce themselves. I looked around frantically, trying to gauge how much damage might be seen from the doorway by someone looking for trouble, and then cast one wry glance heavenward as I headed for the door.

"Rona, dear," said Mrs. Wicker with eyes darting to the apartment's interior, "did you hear that horrible brawl last night? I thought someone was being murdered upstairs. . . . Did it disturb you terribly?"

"Sure I heard it," I replied from behind the door I opened just barely enough to speak through. "I thought the building was going to come apart . . . and you told me this was a quiet place. . . ."

"Well this has *never* happened before. I can't imagine who was responsible. . . . Well, dear, so sorry, and I hope you won't have a bad impression of us. . . ."

Mrs. Wicker walked away, muttering bemusedly under her breath. I shut the door and returned to my scrubbing, muttering under *my* breath, "So this is what fame and fortune are like. . . ."

Sandra, I am happy to report, survived the night; so did Mr. Teen Star. They lived "happily" together for another few months and then went their separate ways. Sandra and I remained friends for many years, but I went out of my way to avoid the adolescent idol after that night.

CHAPTER EIGHT

April, 1960, proved to be a very bad month.

Stacy Templeton (and that's not her real name) was beginning to show cyclical signs of restlessness, and I knew trouble was in the air. I had observed a pattern of affection and disaffection over the two years of our close friendship, but when I got past Stacy's first anniversary test, I convinced myself I was going to be the exception to the rule.

For all of Stacy's spoiled-brat qualities, she was a pretty, graceful woman-child, generous with her warmth and laughter to those she favored and viciously cold to those who fell out of favor. And if it sometimes seemed that *all* her friendships were transient, she would explain that she couldn't help having "a quick boring point."

Stacy's father headed one of the largest theatrical agencies in the country and was extremely well-liked and well-connected.

Clute Sampson (and I won't tell you *his* real name) was a stuntman. He had a lot of brawn and a medium-sized brain which permitted him at times to sound witty. Little did anyone know that he would emerge in the early seventies as the darling of the TV nighttime talk shows and the magazines' favorite sex symbol. Clute was Stacy's first big love after a series of petty romances which went nowhere and left her frustrated. But with Clute things became different. He was extremely clever in his own simian way. He saw Stacy for what she was—a scared, naive little rich girl who was ripe for the plucking. And in three months he plucked her off but good. He fucked her brains out morning, noon, and night. But he wasn't all *that* smart, for he hadn't quite bargained with her father's ability to move a few mountains—not to mention men!

Though sometimes he wanted to slug his daughter for being a spoiled brat, she was still his daughter, and when she began coming home every night crying because Clute wouldn't marry her, he felt compelled to do something for her. He finally did, by putting pressure on his show biz friends to make sure Clute didn't get called as frequently for certain jobs. It didn't take Clute very long to realize what was happening.

During this period Clute had become quite friendly with me and two chaps in Templeton's office. He asked for a summit meeting at my little apartment.

Clute got there first. I offered him a drink, but he declined.

"I'm not in the mood. I'm taking a plane tonight for New Orleans. And I don't like being drunk when I'm flying."

I was about to ask why he was leaving town, when David and Howard arrived. Clute's anxiety was so intense, he wasn't even in the mood for his usual bullshit dialogue.

"You're Stacy's three closest friends," he began, straight off. "I'm in big trouble, guys. Stacy's pressuring for marriage. I'm not ready for marriage. I never wanted to marry her in the first place. I thought she was ready for some kicks and I was willing to give 'em to her. I didn't bargain for her tantrums or her father. You guys have just got to help me. Please. I want out . . . only I don't know how to do it. If I loved Stacy I'd marry her just to get out that way. But I don't. Man, she's even a bad fuck. Lies there like a dead fish. Man, it's bad news." Clute was getting redder and madder as he talked.

I piped up, "But, Clute, why did you lie to her? She told me a thousand times if she didn't tell me once that you begged her to marry you. That all you did was push marriage and that every other word out of your mouth was how much you loved her. Now you try and tell us that none of that is true. Do you lie, Clute?"

"Listen, baby, I never lie. I never told Stacy a thing like that. She made it up in her head. You'll just have to believe that."

"Well, I'm not too sure that I do," I answered angrily.

David now put his two cents in. "Well what is it you want us to do, Clute? You realize you're putting us in a funny position? After all, Howard and I work for Templeton."

"To tell you the truth, guys, I don't know exactly what I want you to do. Just cover for me with Templeton, I guess. Try and explain to him that I never made any promises like the ones Stacy said I did. Get him to believe me and get him off my back. I've got no bread and I've got to get back to work, but the Stuntmen's Association has got me sort of blacklisted. So does the Screen Extra's Guild. It's like my name's poison. Templeton's used his clout pretty good. It's as if I never existed in the first place."

There was suddenly a pathetic pleading tone in Clute's voice. And I began to wonder again just how much Stacy really knew. Maybe Clute wasn't exaggerating and maybe Stacy exaggerated too much; but having been out with the two of them as often as I had, I knew Clute was guilty

of something. I decided it had to be pretending you love
someone when all you really want is to get fucked. It
was all that pillow dialogue men usually hand women
and the foolishness of women wanting to hear it all because they want someone other than mother to love them.

David and Howard agreed to do whatever they could.
I wasn't too sure about my position. I'd have to think
it over. Everyone left.

Two days later I was in Howard's office waiting for
him to take me to a screening, when the phone rang. It
was Clute, long distance from New Orleans. Howard held
the phone out so I could hear.

"Howard, baby. How the hell are you?" Clute asked.

"Super, man. What's up?"

"Baby, I'm free. I'm gettin' married in two weeks to
my old childhood sweetheart!"

Howard and I just looked at each other.

"What did you say?" Howard asked incredulously.

"I'm getting married, man! Ain't that great? Tell anyone
you want. Hear me?"

"What about Stacy? Does she know?"

I whispered to Howard, "Ask him if he's called her."

"Did you call Stacy and tell her?"

There was a silent pause, as if Clute was thinking of
something clever to say. Instead he replied, "No. Why
don't you just ask one of your press agent friends to plant
the story in Army Archerd or Mike Connolly's column
in *The Hollywood Reporter?* Nothing like a little publicity,
I always say."

"Tell him he's crazy!" I whispered loudly to Howard,
who had pressed a button summoning David into his office.
Seeing we were all on the phone, David asked me, "What's
up?"

"Shhhh. Just come here and listen."

Howard was talking. "Honestly, Clute. I don't think it's too grand an idea for one of us to plant the story of your marriage in the trade papers."

"Are you kidding?" David exploded. "Clute and Stacy getting married? It's fantas . . ." I cut David off.

"No stupid. Listen."

But by then Howard had broken the connection and was swiveling around in his chair to face us. He was shaking his head. "Can you believe that bastard?"

"What's going on? Will someone please tell me?" David was annoyed to be the last to know.

"Clute just called," I began answering, "and he's getting married to his childhood sweetheart in New Orleans in two weeks and wants us to have the story planted in one of the trade papers. And furthermore he hasn't told Stacy and wants the papers to be his informant. The bastard."

"Jeeesus Chriiist!"

"Well I don't know about you fellas, but I'm getting out of here. Let's forget the movie tonight, Howard. I'm in no mood. Shit's going to hit the fan tomorrow or in a few days."

"No, let's go to the movie. We'll be able to think more clearly if we take our mind off our problem."

"Listen," said David. "It's *not* our problem. Why should we get involved? Affairs of the heart are dangerous. No one ever wins."

"But Stacy's my best friend. I can't let Clute do that to her. It's awful. How'd you like some girl doing that to you, you rat-fink?"

"Rat-fink? Why're you calling me that?"

"Oh, forget it!" I said, throwing my hands up in the air. "Ah, all you men stink!"

"Keep thinking that way, sweetheart, and you'll wind up without one."

"Well, if they're all like Clute, and you all seem to be, who needs you?" David walked over to me and bent down and kissed me on my cheek, pinching the other side with his fingers. "Cut it out, David," I said, embarrassed. Whenever I got embarrassed I hunched my shoulders up around my ears like a turtle trying to stick its head back into its shell. But David wouldn't stop his teasing and he then grabbed hold of my nose between his two fingers and began pulling. "Stop it, David! Stop! My nose is big enough as it is. You don't have to make it bigger. You want me to look like Pinocchio?"

I was self-conscious about my nose. From every angle, I felt it looked too large for my face. It especially annoyed me when photographers caught me in profile. From that angle I looked like I could hook myself onto a clothesline and hang there with little fear of falling. From the front angle, however, only the tip of my nose seemed too bulbous. Stacy, for a whole year, had tried to get me to have plastic surgery, but until now I had been frightened. Besides, I had no money. It would take at least ten stories at a hundred dollars a story before I could have enough capital to afford the doctor's fee and a little something left over to pay my rent, my car payment, my telephone, my gas and electric bill, water bill and God knew what else if I were to survive such a deal. I thought a lot about it and stood for hours in front of my bathroom mirror wondering what I would look like with a new nose. Would it really make me beautiful? Eventually I decided I didn't *have* to look like Elizabeth Taylor. Maybe just a better-looking Rona Barrett would be good enough. I turned my thoughts to what kind of stories I could write and who would pay me a hundred bucks apiece for them.

At that point in my career, I was getting about forty-five

and fifty dollars a story and the three little columns I wrote for three innocuous movie magazines brought me a big fat two hundred and fifty dollars a month. "And people think in Hollywood you make big money," I would chuckle to myself almost every month when I had to juggle the bills. Sometimes I managed to pay them all, but those months were rare. How I'd muster enough cash for the nose bob was my number one diversion all that winter—next to Stacy and her problem with Clute.

I couldn't concentrate on the movie. I was thinking heavily of Stacy and the rotten Clute and how guys were always far more capable of playing bedroom games than girls were. I was also concerned about the nose bob, and all through the movie I kept playing with my nose, poking it in every direction. I was scheduled for the operation in two days. Stacy had set it up for me. My medical insurance would cover the operation and the hospital stay. The doctor even agreed to cut his fee to practically nothing —$250. He was the kind of man who really enjoyed seeing the psychological effects of cosmetic surgery, and he had a hunch that I needed as much moral support as I could get.

In the morning, after working and worrying all night, I made up my mind there was no way I would allow Stacy to read about Clute's coming marriage in the trade papers. If he didn't have the guts to tell her what he was up to, I would do it for him.

Stacy was not at all grateful for the information. In fact, she became hysterical. "You're lying! You're lying! You're just making it up because you're jealous of Clute and me!"

"Don't be ridiculous, Stacy. Why would I do such a thing? Just ask David and Howard. They'll tell you."

"You better believe I will!" She hung up in a fury.

Two days later, lying in the hospital bed with bandages covering my entire nose and most of my face, I was paid a visit by David, who tried to make with some witty conversation but was obviously disturbed about something.

"How's Stacy?" I asked. "I'm surprised I haven't heard from her by now."

"I guess she's all right," said David.

"What do you mean . . . you guess she's all right?"

"Rona, I've got something to tell you, but I don't know how. And I'm not too sure I should be telling you while you're still in the hospital, but somehow I found myself here this afternoon . . . and I . . . I . . ."

"Okay, out with it," I demanded nasally. I had to talk and breathe through my mouth simultaneously.

"Everything's backfired!" David blurted out. "You shouldn't have called Stacy. That stupid idiot went and called Clute and Clute said he never spoke to you and that you're a liar and that you were only trying to make trouble because you're jealous of his love for Stacy because . . . because . . . you're a *lesbian!*"

I looked up at David. I pulled myself up from the pillow and braced myself on my elbows. "What did you say?"

"You heard me. He accused you of being a les. Says you're really in love with Stacy and don't want her to be happy with a guy."

"David, he's crazy!" I screamed. "He's crazy! I don't even know what he's talking about."

"Well, that isn't all," David continued. "Stacy's now concocting stories to substantiate Clute's accusation. Last night up at Bobby Darin's house Stacy was telling everyone that they shouldn't have anything to do with you.

She said you made a pass at her one night when you were staying over at the Templeton home."

"A pass at her!"

"Yeah. A pass. Said you tried to feel her titties and grab her all over."

I tried to speak but only garbled sounds emerged from my mouth and tears poured out of my eyes and soaked the bandages. Then I started screaming and suddenly blood was coming from my mouth and through the bandages. I was hemorrhaging like a son of a bitch and David panicked and called for a nurse.

The nurse bounded into the room and herself let out a yell, "Oh, my God. What happened!"

David tried to explain, but the nurse wasn't listening. She pressed the emergency button and two other nurses suddenly appeared. I kept screaming. "David! David! It's a lie. I never did it. I never did! Believe me. Why is she saying that? Why? David! David! Do you believe me?"

Another nurse turned to David and asked, "What in the hell is she screaming about?"

"Just fix her up," David answered, walking out of the room. He never could stand the sight of blood.

A few minutes later the surgeon arrived and I was rushed back to the operating room. An artery in my throat had burst, as did one in my nose—a result of my screaming. He sutured the breaks, repacked my nose and bandaged me once again. Luckily no permanent damage was done.

News of my falling out with Stacy Templeton (and subsequently with her parents, who believed their daughter) spread like wildfire, and I became Hollywood's very own Typhoid Mary overnight. All the good-time friends disappeared, my phone practically stopped ringing, and important interviews I'd scheduled were suddenly delayed or canceled. Aside from David, only two friends came to my defense. They were Helen and Beverly Noga. Helen was a personal manager and she handled Johnny Mathis, at the time the nation's number one recording star. She was also very close to the Templetons.

Helen demanded that David bring me to her home to stay when I left the hospital. Helen thrived on righting wrongs, and she came to my defense.

But at the Noga home I found only partial solace. Helen meant well, but every day she would transmit the latest from Stacy, and I found myself retreating to my bed and feeling like I could never escape from it. It was like being glued to the tree when I was five and the kids stood around poking me with their sticks. Helpless. Hopeless. I cried constantly and thought again about killing myself to end the pain and the hurt. I hemorrhaged once more and in the middle of the night an ambulance took me through the quiet streets of Beverly Hills to the Beverly Glen Hospital for two days of repair work.

In the meantime, Helen and Bev contrived a plot to put an end to the whole messy business. Helen thought Bev could telephone Stacy and prod her into spilling the real beans. Stacy wasn't made of the stuff that could endure pressure and if handled right she would have to crack. Helen's intuition paid off and she taped every word Stacy babbled to Bev, including the minutest details of her affair with Clute and how Clute had planted the idea of me being a lesbian. It all seemed so meaningless to Stacy—as if she were discussing a new dress she'd just bought at Jax—that both Helen and Bev wanted to strangle the girl. However, she was a safe three miles away.

The following day, with tape in hand, Helen asked for an appointment to see Max at his office. Before Maxwell could show her to a chair, Helen looked him straight in the eye and said:

"Maxwell, you weak son of a bitch asshole. How you could let your daughter get away with the kind of bullshit she pulls in this town is a disgrace. You're an asshole! And I wanted to be the first to tell you!" She then laid the tape on Templeton and needless to say that was the end of the story. Later she told me all the details.

So that particular nightmare ended for me and I dug up the courage to go out on the town a few nights later.

I kept looking into the mirror. The swelling was going down and the blackness around my eyes was fading. The doctor had done a wonderful job. I almost didn't recognize myself. The Jewish nose was gone, but I dreadfully feared my first social outing. That rotten bitch, Stacy. I started crying, but remembering what the doctor had said about crying wrinkling the nose, I stopped.

So far I've pretty much been able to tell my story chronologically. But about 1961, that stopped being true.

My life started to be like the sideshow baseball dodger. "Hit Rona Barrett and win a prize!" fate seemed to be saying. Because everywhere I turned, something was coming at me. Not just one or two problems but three or four or five big ones all at once.

Not that I'm trying to cop a plea. Some of them were of my own making.

No matter what new crises came at me, though, there were a couple of constant ones. The first revolved around my career. If I wrote what I really knew, I'd hurt people, make enemies. If I didn't, I wouldn't build a following. I didn't know what to do. I tried to come out with the best of both worlds by digging for "good" items that were so exclusive people couldn't help noticing them. Still, I wasn't making enough progress and it plagued me.

My other constant problem was in the romance department. Surgery had done all it could for me. But men were still mainly attracted to me for what power I had, not for Rona Barrett the woman. One day, I decided to try and save that once and for all.

I'd heard about Louise Long for some time.

She'd modeled Marlene Dietrich's face from round to gaunt. She changed the shape of Mitzi Gaynor's legs from ordinary to eye-catching. She'd made Kim Novak from a Polish cow into an American princess. It was hard to believe that someone could actually remold bodies *without* a surgeon's knife. But seeing was believing, and I'd seen some of these superstars before Louise had gotten hold of them.

I went to see her.

There were only two roadblocks. The time. The cost. Louise worked between the hours of 3:00 A.M. and 12:00 noon, and had only the 4:00 and 5:00 A.M. spots open (unless I wanted to wait until the following spring). And she cost what in those days was a lot of money for a "massage." More important, she required you take a minimum of ten. I scraped together enough money for the first few, figuring I'd get the rest as I went along. On a Thursday at 5:00 in the morning I arrived for my first visit with Louise.

When I finally found the address, I figured that the press agents of Mitzi Gaynor and Marlene Dietrich and Kim Novak and all the rest had put one over on Rona Barrett. Anyone working out of a place like this would be lucky to eat three squares a day, let alone mold the girl next door into Miss Superstar of the Screen!

None of the doors closed properly. There were cobwebs

hanging from the ceilings—literally. Old rickety tables were everywhere but all of them put together wouldn't have been worth two bucks at a garage sale.

It looked like some second-rate Mexican abortion basement.

But the minute I saw Louise Long, the tables looked like Paul McCobb. She was a giant and every inch gorgeous. *She must know something,* I thought to myself.

I'll never forget the first words she said to me: "You are *really* beautiful, Rona. It doesn't show yet, but that's *my* job. I'm going to *make* it show. I'm going to bring out your beauty."

She guided me to an inner room which was different than the rest of the house, told me to remove all my clothes and lie upon a kind of combination couch-examining table. When she began, I had second thoughts again. God, it hurt. She grabbed at every fat pocket on my body—and there were many. She first began with the fat pockets on my hips. She pinched and squeezed them and I could literally feel her flushing the fat away. In between the pinches, squeezes, and rubbing, she slapped with cupped hands the area she had just been mutilating. She repeated the process all over my body. Then I spent fifteen or twenty minutes on electrical machines similar to Relaxacisors, but stronger and more painful. They toned the muscles.

I think it was the most physically painful hour I ever spent in my life. And to think there would be at least nine more like it! I moaned. I groaned. But I stayed with it. What choice did I have? I couldn't keep associating with the most beautiful women in the world, day in and day out, and be the ugly duckling. But it would all be worth it if . . .

The results were remarkable. They showed after one treatment. After nine more, *there was an unbelievable transformation.* It took Louise longer to reshape my face than any other part of my body, but eventually it all worked.

Now I felt I could totally wage the battle to climb higher. I could become one of them. I went to Louise for nearly a year straight, and saw her intermittently for years after until she died.

I began to look like a star. The proof of the pudding was my first big interview, after the first ten treatments. It was with Hugh O'Brian, who was making it big with his Wyatt Earp series. The only problem was that Hugh was becoming Wyatt Earp off the set as well as on, six-shooter always poised for action.

He met me next to his swimming pool. Naturally, he was wearing only trunks. In the middle of my third question, I looked up from my pad of paper to find . . . just Hugh.

"What do you say, beautiful?" he said.

"I say put your bathing suit back on," I answered.

But I was frankly flattered.

And I let him know it. We not only parted friends, but I got a better interview out of him.

Not that there wasn't a hard moment after I asked Hugh to dress. Like every other gorgeous, "masculine," dashing idol I'd known, underneath his handsome sun-bronzed skin Hugh was just a little boy who wanted to revert to the world he'd known at ten or six or maybe even when he was nursing at his mother's breast, a world where he was the only male on the face of the earth! Or, at least, so far and away the most important male that any woman who was worth it would fall at his feet. For years, he'd pretty well harnessed some of that feeling.

He'd had to. But once Hugh had made it—and as Wyatt Earp—he could really let loose and be the god to women he'd always known he was anyway.

But I understood that. I even found it magnetic at times. Partly because *I* had the same thing inside me. But I had something else, too, something that would never let me be a part of that scene. Some of it no doubt was my middle-class Jewish background. But I honestly think a lot of it was my sense of fair play. The Hugh O'Brians could afford to be interviewed in the nude. But it just wasn't kosher to write about their pranks and their affairs when I was playing and sleeping with them myself. Just as I could only write about their problems when I wasn't laying my own troubles on them.

So, I stayed a virgin—for quite a while anyway. And because they never got "into" me, just like in New York, I was able to get into them all the more. They leaned on me. I had hardly an enemy in those early years. There was hardly a party in Hollywood to which I wasn't invited. Though I finally did have a "love affair" with a man that put me through daily hell, hardly any of them knew the first thing about it. Just as no one knew I was once a cripple. And only those who had met me more than once the first year knew that I was apple-cheeked, warty, scarred, Semitic and ugly. They only knew to call with their crises and their plugs . . . Bobby Darin, George Hamilton, Connie Stevens, Troy Donahue, Frankie Avalon, Fabian, Bobby Sherman, Roger Smith, Ann-Margret, Stuart Whitman, Carroll Baker, Bob Wagner, Natalie Wood, Nick Adams, Diane Baker and so many others. "You're our leader," Darin said to me one night when a bunch of us left for Cyrano's, the *in* coffee house on the Strip.

And in a way I was. It made other columnists, even

the biggies, begin to wonder what my "technique" was. But it was *no* technique.

The stories I came up with first, the "items" I got for my column before anyone else, more often than not were simply a result of my being with the people—or with people who intimately knew the people—to whom things were happening. I always weighed my words carefully, never broke a confidence, never wrote to hurt anybody, believe it or not.

Oh, there were formal affairs and parties and arranged interviews, of course, which could be pretty superficial if you let them. But I tried never to let them. If I sensed that the scene was going that way, I'd simply walk up to someone and say, "Do you make a hundred thousand a year yet?" or "How good a fuck are you?" or "Have you ever attempted suicide?" or "What did you really think of your half-assed co-star in your last picture?" Needless to say, I seldom got answers to those questions. But after asking one of them, they didn't dare give me any pap or press agentry.

So those early sixties were the outwardly uneventful yet absolutely necessary years in my career when I learned my craft better and better, from how to verify a story six ways instead of three, to learning how to absolutely protect myself against libel, to simply how to write better. Those were the years when I made innumerable valuable contacts, not just among performers or presidents, but with the heads of the studios and corporations who put them where they were ("Actors come and go," I was once quoted as saying, "but executives are forever.")

In my own little way I was beginning to be known as the queen of the fan magazines.

But I was still waiting for that one big break. At long

last, an opening came. *Motion Picture Magazine,* one of the top in its field, was looking for a new, bright column to join Hedda Hopper's more staid one.

Jack Podell, MP's editor, and his associate, Larry Thomas, had watched me grow on the scene, had read my columns monthly in the three new magazines Bessie Little was publishing. Bessie and I had made up.

But now one of the biggest and the best had finally asked me to join them. It was time to move on. It was hard for me to break with Bessie, but it would have been harder not to.

Motion Picture gave me one stipulation, however.

If I were to become a successful columnist, once a month I had to take out after someone.

That was the one condition.

I was chomping at the bit to say yes. But how could I? "These people are my friends," I told Podell over the phone.

"Every *one* of them?"

I paused. Five years ago, I might have said, "Yes, *every one of them.*" Oh, Warren Beatty hadn't been any bargain and Eddie Fisher had hurt me—but not intentionally. Should I want to hurt their careers just because I didn't think much of them as people?

Surprisingly, I found myself seriously considering it. Maybe it was partly revenge against those who had hurt me, partly rationalization because I wanted to reach the top so badly. But I know that part of it was what it had always been with me: *Simply to tell it like it was.*

I believed in the message of Hollywood: *Heroes and heroines, life as a dramatic struggle.* But I wasn't going to uphold false idols or fake the drama. If a moving, inspiring singer like Eddie Fisher turned out to be shallow and prejudiced, if a charismatic, brilliant actor like Warren Beatty revealed himself as a spoiled brat, or Marlo Thomas as a ballbuster, or Cary Grant, as he-man as he is, really being more of a mother than a father to his daughter Jennifer, that didn't change the truly beautiful people from being beautiful, didn't detract from those who strove to make the achievements inside themselves as great as those the world saw. No one reaches the top without *something* unique. What was wrong with letting the world see both sides, all facets?

"I'll do it," I heard myself saying.

And so I added a facet to my own career. The Rona Barrett of whom Johnny Carson said, "She doesn't need a steak knife. Rona cuts her food with her tongue." My life was more a series of multiple crises than ever before. Little did I realize that the stories I will now tell you would affect me in such a way that in the end Hollywood's alleged "Big Mouth" would in reality be one of Hollywood's great recluses.

My first crisis involved Frankie Avalon. Those of you who are within a few years of my age will no doubt know Frankie's name. If you're in your teens, chances are you don't. It's no loss.

At one, with my parents.

*I was always
falling down and walking around
with band-aids on my knees.*

With my baby sister, Marcia.

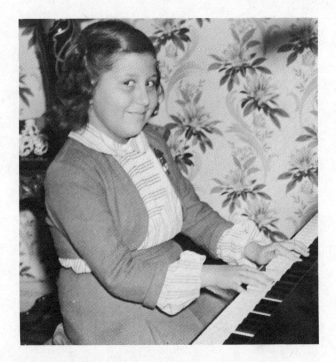

I was thrilled
when Harry Belafonte
invited me to sit on his lap.

My sweet sixteen party. Steve Lawrence was my guest of honor.

Bob Evans was always a lady-killer . . . and a very good friend.

With Troy Donahue at the height of his career.

Connie Stevens and me—with our old noses.

Out with my parents for the first time with my new nose.

Though my face was still swollen, I went to Bobby Darin's opening at the now-defunct Cloisters.

With Johnny Mathis.

With Peter Brown and Peggy Castle on the set of "The Lawman."

My Claudette Colbert picture.

With the late Edward G. Robinson

Bill and I were married on September 22, 1973.

Just a few minutes after Goldie Hawn won her Oscar.

With Carol Burnett

With Hugh Hefner

With Kirk Douglas

The late Veronica Lake, Mae West and me at a party I gave for Veronica. They had never met before.

CHAPTER NINE

There is probably no reporter who knows the Frankie Avalon story better than I do. I was there from the very beginning, on my way to becoming the "Queen of the Fan Magazines," as someone had dubbed me. And in 1958–59, the fan mags were still the most influential periodicals to build and make stars.

I had heard about Bob Marcucci. From Philadelphia, he had started a company called Chancellor Records. He was riding high with a big hit, "With All My Heart," by a then unknown singer, Jodi Sands. Word spread fast that Marcucci was a promotional genius. Someone suggested that it would be a good idea if we met. The meeting took place in 1958. By '59 our friendship had blossomed into an enduring one.

In the meantime, Marcucci had the idea that the country was ready for a big teenage singing idol. He was out to find and build one.

He heard of Frankie Avalon from the kids on the street.

Actually, Avalon had developed a reputation as a terrific trumpet player. One day, Marcucci turned up at Avalon's house. He told Frankie what he was looking for. Avalon, who was earning eighty dollars a week playing trumpet with a group called Rocco and the Saints, told Marcucci he *had* what Bob wanted. There was a kid in the group who sang real well. Marcucci made an appointment to hear the kid at the place where the group was currently playing. It was a little "joint" in New Jersey. The joint has since been destroyed by fire.

Marcucci did not sign the kid. He signed another youngster who had sung a number that fateful night. Marcucci was convinced he had found the teenager he had been searching for.

Frankie Avalon.

Aside from a record contract, Marcucci also signed Avalon to a personal management contract. Thus it was with dramatic suddenness that Frankie's name began to spread all around the country and, soon, around the whole world.

A recording star had been born.

Marcucci went on a search for another teenage idol. This one he planned to build into a motion picture star. He knew, however, the fastest way to accomplish it was again through the musical route. And so, one day, he came across this good-looking, sexy young kid sitting on a stoop. The kid was no more than fifteen years old. Bob looked at the kid and just like they do in the movies, asked: "Can you sing?"

The kid said: "No."

"Well," said Marcucci, "I'll teach you to sing. Make you a star, in fact."

The kid's name was Fabian Forte, which Marcucci shortened to the arresting Fabian. Bob was now on his way to building his second teenage idol. Because of his good looks, Fabian caught on even faster than Avalon.

It was at this period that I entered the Marcucci picture. Bob's press people came to me for assistance in building Fabe and Frank through my columns in the movie mags.

I liked both kids at first meeting. They were groovy. Frankie was sexy and witty, at times, though kind of an emaciated Burt Reynolds. As for Fabe, I really loved him. We were like brother and sister together. Though he didn't have much formal education, there was something interestingly intuitive about him. He absorbed new things like a sponge. By the time he was eighteen, he had become a walking university. Fabe couldn't read enough good books or be around enough intelligent people who could teach him. All he wanted to do was learn.

Frankie, on the other hand, was interested in eating everything so it didn't eat him first.

When the gang moved to Hollywood, they rented a glamorous house above the Sunset Strip on Pine Tree Place. It became the hangout for just about every young star in Hollywood. And I became den mother. There were very few moves Marcucci made without consulting me. Not that he needed my advice. It was simply that he knew there were few people "out there" he could trust with his innermost secrets. As a result, we developed the kind of friendship many people envy and often try to destroy. We became each other's pillars of strength.

Even the boys looked toward me for advice. Though I was a columnist and a reporter, I rarely reported what went on inside Pine Tree Place. If I was to become a success I couldn't suppress *everything*. I knew it would be impossible for me to have many really intimate "star" friends. So I had a larger circle of dozens with whom I was a "friend" friend. I would report their personal activities, but never to the point of permanently injuring their careers. My "inner" clan, however, I only boosted, protected like family. They were Frankie, Fabe, Marcucci, Nancy Sinatra, Tommy Sands, Jimmy Darren, Bobby Darin, and Mickey Callan. There were other young stars like George Hamilton, Paul Anka, Nick Adams, who *thought* they were members of that group, but they weren't.

Now, however, only one member of the "family" still remains: Bob Marcucci.

Nancy and Tommy divorced. The divorce made Nancy finally turn on me. Tommy Sands had a breakdown and moved to the Islands.

Jimmy Darren decided to stick with the Sinatra camp. As did Mickey Callan.

Bobby Darin married Sandra Dee, who could never understand my closeness to Bobby and during that marriage our friendship became very shaky. After they divorced, Bobby and I picked up where we once left off—until his untimely death.

As for Fabe, his breakup with Marcucci was the only one which was absolutely necessary. They had grown *too* close. But it made me sad, so sad, to lose Fabe. I miss him a great deal.

As for Frankie, there was something about Avalon I had always found disturbing. I was never sure if he had a sincere bone in his body. He was like a prostitute at heart. If you had the right price, you had him. I could tell from his background that he'd been raised with very narrow-minded attitudes. Of course, we can all overcome our backgrounds.

Frankie didn't. His parents had grown up believing that Jews had purple horns. He did, too. And as far as Negroes were concerned, he was always saying, "Get dem _____ away from me!" Of course, he always accompanied this with a little smile on his lips. But I felt he meant it. I stuck up for him anyway, if not for his remarks.

And so, when big trouble came his way in July of 1961, at the height of his career, I was there, along with Mar-

cucci, to protect Frankie. We protected him for almost
two years. Then suddenly, *all* the fat hit the fire! With
a blaze!

One morning the headline in the *Los Angeles Herald-
Examiner* screamed: FRANKIE AVALON NAMED IN
PATERNITY SUIT!

For two years—two dreadful years—Marcucci and I had
been living a nightmare. Because in those days, paternity
suits were the kind of clothing from which careers were
stripped naked. And I had suffered more than Bob, because
I was the one who had been living on the West Coast
and had been relegated the responsibility of concealing
the suit.

The story began in July of 1961. I had written an item
about two girls, who, for nearly a week, lived in a car
outside of Avalon's home. When Frankie or his parents,
who often visited him from Philadelphia, weren't there,
the girls would sneak down to his pool and bathe themselves! Or sometimes go to a nearby restaurant to freshen
up. They ate, drank, slept, and lived in their old car, parked
directly across from the house. When people would ap-
proach, they'd slide under the front seat so no one would
see them. Every once in a while, when Avalon arrived
home, a bobbing head would appear.

At first, Frankie paid no attention. Then he thought
he was seeing things. When strange doorbell ringing would
startle the household at all hours of the day, but no one
would ever be there, he really began to wonder.

It was finally Frankie's mother who became suspicious
enough of the car parked in about the same spot for so
long that she notified police. They came to investigate.
The girls weren't in the car when the men in blue arrived.
They had gone down the hill to the restaurant. Upon their

return, they cleverly told the police they were just two
pledges to a sorority, whose initiation was to sleep and
eat outside a star's home and not let the star discover
what was going on!

Today they would be called "groupies," young teenagers
whose prime occupation is to make it with some star in
a singing group and then brag about it. Even if they had
to travel halfway across the country or park outside of
his house for a month to do it.

It wasn't until the end of June that a frantic telephone
call was made to Chancellor Records. An hysterical little
girl wanted to know how she could reach Frankie; it was
a matter of life or death.

The call was switched to Bob Marcucci.

He asked the girl what she wanted. She refused to reveal
her predicament, but insisted she *had* to talk to Frankie.

Somehow, she then obtained Frankie's private number
at home in New Jersey and, as fate would have it, he
answered the telephone himself. Groupie was pregnant,
and she accused Frankie of being the father.

Avalon panicked. He couldn't even remember the girl!
He had had so many affairs. Was she one of them? He
quickly collected his wits and said he would call her back.
He called Marcucci. Frantically, they tried to put the
pieces together. Avalon's whole world was at stake. He
had his first big South American tour coming up, an
impending film, new records, television appearances—the
works.

Frankie pushed the panic button even more when he
remembered. He had gone to a big party, gotten slightly
over-served and, as he was about to enter his home, a
young girl rushed up and threw her arms around his neck,
begging him to come and sit with her in her car. He did.
More than sat.

I was the only close friend Frankie and Bob had on the Coast and was immediately called. Bob was going to make a secret trip to California with Frankie's attorney and both men would be meeting with Groupie's attorney. Whether or not Frankie was the father, they couldn't take a chance. By the time they arrived, Bob wanted me to have found out everything I could about the girl.

I did. A few days later I came face to face with Groupie. She wasn't particularly attractive. It almost figured. A girl's looks never mattered to Frankie, so long as she was willing and able. She was terribly frightened, however, and I felt sorry for her even though my loyalty was to Frankie.

During the course of that first conference, Groupie said she really didn't want to cause any problems for him. All she wanted was to have his baby, have Frankie pay for the hospital expenses and nothing more. She swore on her life that no one would ever know where the money came from or that she was raising Frankie Avalon's child.

It was a touchy situation. This girl obviously wasn't an ordinary teenager with a fixation on a movie star.

So it was decided to take the "nuisance" route. If Groupie needed friendly advice she could always call on me at any time of the day or night. If she needed money, she'd get that from Marcucci. *Whatever* she needed, we would try and give her. Because of *one* thing we were absolutely convinced.

She was going to give birth to this baby.

In December of 1961, Groupie had a little girl.

A few days later, I spoke with her, asked her how she had registered at the hospital. She said she registered under her own name and that the birth certificate stated the father was a sailor with some long-sounding foreign name. Somehow, I didn't believe her. She sensed my suspicion and cried out: "Don't you believe me? I swear, I'd never hurt Frankie! *Swear!*"

I checked.

The baby's birth certificate read: Frank E. Avallone, not as long-sounding or foreign as we would have liked.

I immediately notified Bob Marcucci of the events. We both knew it wouldn't be long before Groupie did more. She really didn't want to hurt Frankie. But her desire to let the world know she had Frankie Avalon's baby was just too strong for her to keep down!

Soon, possibly on some bad advice from those surrounding Groupie in her loneliness, she began to have other strong desires. She needed a used car. I rented her a small compact in my name, which I paid for, and was later reimbursed by Marcucci.

A few weeks later, she returned the compact in favor of a Cadillac. We only found this out when the rental bill came in. Then came a "request" for apartment rent. We were in too deep to refuse. Before we knew it, she had taken a new apartment in the exclusive Sunset Strip area. It was double trouble: The big monthly money wasn't even as important as her broken promise that she would stay away from the Hollywood glitter.

Yet I still don't feel she wanted to hurt Frankie. I think her obsessive love for him—which couldn't be satisfied—was simply erupting in other forms. The proof was a series of semihysterical telephone calls she began making. Not only to me, but to Frank's lawyer in Philadelphia. And to Bob Marcucci. They came at strange hours of the day and night. They ranged from Groupie making new wild demands to asking about Frankie's whereabouts and even threatening his life. On one such hysterical occasion in the wee hours of the morning, Groupie went on a literal telephone rampage, called everyone from Frankie's childhood sweetheart (whose name she recalled from a magazine article I wrote) to his sister, and, finally, Frankie himself.

The next day, Avalon's advisors phoned me from Philadelphia asking what in the hell happened. I called Groupie, who confessed she had been drinking, that all she wanted was to hear Frankie's voice. She promised it would never happen again.

To keep her promise, she had to revert to making more demands.

"My car doesn't have automatic seats! . . . Frankie's money was a day late in coming! . . . My baby is sick and needs an operation. . . . Get me a check immediately! . . ." Frantically, Bob and I complied with all her demands. A few weeks later, in a La Cienega restaurant, I bumped into her, looking like a new woman.

This was a fashionably coiffed, slick chick. Not only was her hair different but she had a new nose! "Where did the money for that come from?" I asked. I hadn't been born yesterday.

It didn't faze her one bit.

Hardly an evening went by but at 2:00 or 3:00 in the morning Groupie was calling me on my most private number, making endless demands. I was becoming a nervous wreck. It was obvious we'd made a mistake. We should have let the cards fall where they may the first day she called us.

Groupie's last demand was to meet Frankie face to face for one final time. Reluctantly, the meeting was arranged. She promised to come alone. The meeting place was to be my apartment, late at night. Groupie, however, did *not* come alone. With her was the baby—up way past her bedtime. I thought Frankie would collapse when he saw the child.

We somehow got through the meeting but it wasn't enough. On January 9, 1963, Groupie could hold out no longer. She went to the *Los Angeles Herald-Examiner* and spilled her guts—right after Frankie had announced his forthcoming marriage to a Los Angeles girl named Kay Udilla Deibel, a "socialite" to whom I'd introduced him only a few weeks previous to their surprise engagement. On January 19 they were to be married in church. Their first child arrived several months before their first anniversary.

Two weeks after their marriage, Marcucci and I were out of Frankie's life. It was as if we had never even been there in the first place. *We* were a threat to what Kay hoped to make of Frankie Avalon. He was not only going to be a giant star but, with her "society" connections, would conquer the best of both worlds.

Frankie figured he didn't need me and Marcucci any more now that the Groupie story was out. Now that he was nearing the pinnacle.

That was the beginning of the end for Frankie Avalon. Without Marcucci and his genius promotion mind behind Avalon, there was no more Frankie Avalon. He never existed. But while he did, Frankie was a full-time job for me. It wasn't until much later that I wrote one small item.

Frankie Avalon's lawsuit against his manager and former friend, Bob Marcucci, hits the court this April. Avalon will try to prove that he doesn't owe Marcucci $40,000 in past commissions . . . that he was just a *poor* little boy, who was taken advantage of. . . . Well,

Avalon *was* poor—till Marcucci found him and made him a millionaire!

After that, I was out of Frankie's life for good, too.

I was really into writing for *Motion Picture* but *that* became a box, too. A box I had to break out of.

I felt as if my career was at a standstill again. The fan magazines were getting God awful. Stars were starting *not* to want to see themselves in them! The only way I could *really* have permanent power was to get a syndicated newspaper column and compete directly with Graham, Hopper, and Winchell. But the big syndicates each had their own heavyweight. Finally I arranged an interview with the head of Bell-McClure, John Osenenko. Bell was Drew Pearson's and Sheila Graham's syndicate, and Big John was quietly looking for a stand-in to replace Graham in case she ever got too far out of line.

I got lucky with John. It took me over a year to convince him to hire me. Several things finally made that happen. First, Alex Freeman, a New York columnist, now dead, had spoken highly of me. Second, John's wife liked me, according to John. And finally, he admitted his wife and teenage sons religiously read my columns in *Motion Picture!*

I was hired to become a syndicated columnist for Bell-McClure, a subsidiary of the powerful North American Newspaper Alliance, which distributed Sheila Graham and the great Drew Pearson, who eventually bought the syndicate and indirectly became my boss. My success, however, was again *not* instant. Osenenko met with many obstacles. Newspapers were dying around the country. Editors were cutting back. No one believed the era of Hollywood would continue. They were waiting for all the ladies to die, and that would be it.

But I refused to believe them. I prodded Osenenko till he was blue in the face. I felt like Attila the Hun.

Two years later, my column appeared in one hundred and twenty-five newspapers. I had a greater readership than some of the biggies and a bank account which every week recorded a fat seventy-five dollars. I couldn't believe it.

Neither could anyone else. Unless stars or press agents can read their name or their clients' names in a local outlet, you don't mean a damn in Hollywood.

I didn't mean a damn in Hollywood. God, I had worked my buns off, only to discover press agents bought my column from out-of-town papers and fed my items to the biggies. I kept reading my material, days after it was in print, in Kilgallen's and Connolly's columns.

Osenenko worked his two hundred and fifty pounds ten hours a day for me alone some days, just to break through, to crash that one big New York or L.A. or Chicago paper that would start dozens of others falling in line like dominos for us.

But it never happened.

The competition had every key metropolitan daily locked up tighter than Doris Day's professional virginity. The world *was* changing. Yet the newspapers and magazines which dealt with it—to say nothing of good old careful TV—were afraid to change with it, to feed the public the kind of news they were willing to accept but in a style that would be denoted as circa 1960s. American morals were changing drastically. Hollywood was changing drastically—on every front. But every time I tried to report a story of this nature, I found Rosie, my editor, had penciled it out. In the margin he'd write: "Really,

Rona, this kind of story is not necessary." This kind of story usually dealt with the increasing use of marijuana at parties or a prediction that a number of female stars were seriously thinking of having babies out of wedlock. Rosie, may he rest in peace, didn't think that kind of story was good for the country, let alone Hollywood. I never disagreed with Rosie, but if that's what was happening, that's what I had to write about.

I persevered. It was during this time that I began teaching myself a half-dozen different ways to write an item. The "in" campy folk began reading between my lines. I think they have always remained my biggest fans. In the end, the big stories Rosie had blue-penciled were in print—not the way I had originally penned them, but disguised. Even my "drug" story saw ink. It went like this:

> One of Hollywood's top young producers—a bachelor—opened his new mansion for a gathering which will long be remembered as one of the great "hi-lites" in party giving. Everyone felt so solicitous, thanks to their host's graciousness, that everyone greeted everyone else with a "Hi"!

Rosie thought that was a sweet item. In the 1960s, he had no idea how *sweet* it was!

I worked harder than ever. Now I had a war going on two fronts: It wasn't going to be enough to just find a niche for myself. The niche had to be established along with the new tide. If not, I'd go nowhere. I worried a lot. I thought about my competitors.

There was Hedda. She was the one who continued

living in the thirties; Louella kept becoming more senile;
Earl Wilson kept smiling at everybody; Kilgallen kept
protecting her "What's My Line?" TV career at the ex-
pense of her journalism. My insides, that gut feeling, told
me that if I didn't fight, the field would die even faster.

But Walter Winchell and Hedda Hopper wouldn't have
to worry about it. They'd already been at the top of the
heap for two generations. They'd had theirs. And anyway,
they'd still have the power to branch out in whatever
direction was next, because they were *at* the pinnacle,
almost seemed to own it.

All but those at the very top would fall to the very
bottom when the bottom fell out. I knew it was coming
soon. I worked harder than ever, slaved, watching for a
possible breakthrough, like the quarterback waits a whole
afternoon for that split second of daylight when he can
loft the ball half the length of the field into the fingertips
of a racing receiver and pull the game out in the final
seconds.

It didn't come.

The clock was running out on me.

Another year passed. Then another. I was going to be
thirty years old!

Almost all the people I'd sat around with, grown up
with, coffee-housed with, listened to, laughed with, cried
over in New York and now in Hollywood had become
superstars or on the verge of it. Paul Newman and Sidney
Poitier became the white and black idols of the country.
. . . Shelley Winters had as many Academy Awards and
Emmys as she had husbands. . . .

Yes, I was "successful." I was "up there." But I very
definitely was not on top. I wanted to be at Mt. Somewhere. I wanted to . . . look down on all the rest . . .

as many, many years ago they'd all looked down on me.

Who *cares!*

I'll worry about it later, I answered myself. *Once I get there. All I know now is that I want it. Want it more than anything else. Want it so bad that nothing else matters if I don't get it!*

I didn't know—couldn't know—that every frustration, every extra hour I worked when others were partying or sleeping, was readying me, readying me to soon perch on the precipice of a fame even larger than *I* had imagined. Larger than life. All I understood was that I couldn't stand being anything *but* Number One and that one of these days I actually wouldn't be able to stand it.

I didn't know what I would do then.

But now what I did—in whatever hours he cruelly made available to me—was to stay and stay and stay and stay and stay and stay and stay in an incredibly self-destructive relationship with the devil in a man's body.

CHAPTER TEN

How do you write about a man with whom you spent almost eleven years? A man who had hurt me more than all the rest of the hurts of my life put together.

When I began with Marc (and that's not his real name, of course), I never dreamed it would end up that way. Of course, I guess no one does. But in my case it really might have been a bit different.

Because I was going to try so hard.

I'd waited so long.

But when I laid eyes on Marc, I knew all the waiting and the surgery and the body molding were worth it.

He had every quality I wanted in a man: physical perfection (which I valued too much because of my own previous imperfections), intelligence, ambition, boldness, and several other important ingredients, like character—or at least so it seemed.

The trouble is you don't see all of the inside as fast as you see the outside. Within a short time I realized that he was always slightly perverted, slightly mean, slightly unreal, slightly sick—a bastard.

Is it true that into every woman's life, in order for her to reach the pinnacle of her womanhood, must walk that one all-time bastard?

Mine nearly killed me! But for close to eleven years I thought I loved him. I tingled whenever he touched me, whenever he even came into the room. I worshipped him while he tortured me for worshipping him.

And, like so many women before me, I refused to fully face it.

For some inexplicable reason, I remained loyal to him. It was as if I had to remain crippled in one form or another. Marc helped me to do so until . . .

But let's begin at the beginning.

January, 1962.

First, he was simply gorgeous.

He was the cream of the WASP crop. To Rona Burstein from Queens—and I would always be Rona Burstein from Queens to some degree—he was all the physical things I wanted in a man. His face and coloring made Jack and Bobby Kennedy look pallid. Big blue eyes. White-on-white teeth. Long athletic legs. Rippling muscles. And a fastidious, immaculate dresser who seemed to have that impeccable instinct that made his exquisite body surge right through his clothes.

There's a Jewish word for it. *Geshmak.*

Marc was perfection, from the top of his head to the tip of his toes. And it's important. Don't ever let a woman tell you it's not. Maybe some can get past the body to what's inside. But I wanted both. And the body is what hung me up first. Marc had a body like no man I've seen before or since, and that includes all the Burt Lancasters, Paul Newmans, Charlton Hestons, and Joe Namaths.

And he seemed to be perfection mentally, too.

Marc was bright, so bright. Most important, he was ambitious. He was the most ambitious man I've ever met. He was just in his early thirties when I found him. He was "about to do it." I was twenty-four. His dreams!

"I'm not going to build just an empire, Rona," he told

me the second night. "I'm going to build a *dynasty*."

I had been with the superambitious for a decade. I'd seen the Eddie Fishers (and he didn't hold a candle to Marc) perched atop the pinnacle in just three or four years. Marc would go higher, and he wouldn't perch. He'd stay.

And that, even more than the body, was what I wanted most in a man, because *I* was *so* ambitious. I needed a man who would surpass me, so I wouldn't threaten him, so I could look up to him. *That* excited me more than *anything*.

But if Marc hadn't been quite as ambitious or as superb looking, he *still* would have turned me on more than any man I'd ever met.

He was far and away the most sexual human being I'd ever encountered, or ever will. He was *too* sexual. Because whatever he wasn't doing in the world, he made up for in bed, as the years passed and the empire, let alone the dynasty, failed to form.

The first evening we met, Marc didn't tell me about his worldly ambitions. He told me about his sexual ambitions—to get into my pants. I wouldn't let him. So he took my girlfriend home instead. She called me at three in the morning, sounding like her life had been changed. "Rona," she whispered in a hoarse voice, "I never knew what it could be like till tonight. He's got an organ like an elephant's, and does he ever know how to use it!"

That stimulated me, but it angered me, too. I didn't let him touch me for months after that. Not even to hold an arm getting out of a car.

And *that* fascinated *him*.

He pursued me then as I'd never known anybody to go after a girl, even in crazy, extreme Hollywood. It still disturbed me what he did that first night, but I looked upon it as a test for me, as something he'd done *only* to show me how much he wanted me. Yes, I'd since heard how incomparably he'd performed with a number of other stars and starlets, but why not? Now I was here. Now it was only Rona. In an instant it was a nightmare. We never did make love when he tried to. Instead, he whimpered himself to sleep, telling me that I was the only woman in the world who had meant anything to him. I was the best friend he ever had. I always would be. I didn't know what impotency really meant at that time. I only knew that I loved this man more than life itself. He seemed to love me, too. His kisses—they reached me down to the bottom of my soles and soared me to the Bells of St. Mary.

We finally did consummate our relationship. But it wasn't until years later, on a New Year's day afternoon, after Marc had guzzled an entire bottle of Dom Pérignon.

It was everything I dreamed it to be. He was beautiful. He was magnificent. He was tender.

I wondered why it had taken him so many years to do what should have happened so naturally so many years before. I wondered why I had permitted myself to wait so long for this moment of great ecstasy, causing me for years to live in a constant state of depression because I could not get the man I loved, and who claimed to love me, to make love to me. To marry me. To want me the way I kept hearing he wanted other women. I drove myself sick. I convinced myself it was because Marc was too good-looking and I was just too plain. I wasn't pretty enough for him. He needed someone beautiful and all the women I ever heard he was with were beautiful. And then I convinced myself that my real problem was that I wasn't successful enough for Marc. If he were going to become a senator from California, for which he was being groomed when I met him, he needed someone far more distinguished than myself.

I dreamed. If only I were Louella, or Hedda, or Winchell. I'd be powerful. I'd be strong. I'd be a someone. God, he would want me then. *Wouldn't he?*

No matter how I drove myself, it was to little avail. You're probably asking yourself: why in the hell didn't she confront this man and ask him what the problem was? You're right, dear reader. I just didn't have the guts. I was afraid of the answer. I didn't want to hear it. Having only half of him was better than having nothing. That's what I kept telling myself. And in the end I was so convincing I could not believe how many years had gone by. How many years I had allowed him to torture me and permitted myself to be tortured.

That was the "script" for our relationship. Every episode I ever knew with him, every scene we played together, was verging on ecstasy one instant, plunging into torture the next.

Marc was like an emotional, sexual cannibal. I later learned he was that way in business, too. When I found out that Marc really wasn't an independent, forceful empire-builder, I began to lose respect for him. Yet long before that, I lost almost all respect for *myself* because of our relationship. Just as he outcharmed, outwitted and outconfronted men into lending or giving him the money to invest in his own interests, so he outcharmed, outwitted and outconfronted me out of my emotional lifeblood. He drank the guts of my soul like a vampire drinks blood or a computer drinks information. Then, in the wee hours of the morning, leaving me almost empty, he would take my psychic guts back with him wherever he went so he would never have to feel the emptiness of himself. And because I'd never stopped believing there was a pinnacle and that it was worth reaching, that despite all the ugliness in us and around us, life could be beautiful, because I'd been to the depths in my own life and could still see the heights, he wanted me more than anyone, wanted me in a way he'd never wanted another woman.

I knew that Marc would never run out of the taking, but that one day I would wake up and have nothing more to give. Unlike the pathetically crippled five-year-old who learned to withstand the jeers of her peers, unlike the Pollyannaish thirteen-year-old who thought a loveless person like Eddie Fisher could give her the ocean-deep love she needed, a twenty-six or twenty-eight or thirty-year-old Rona would have nothing left with which to fight, nothing to crawl to so that I could stand one more time, if I let this man keep filling his voracious needs through me. When you live for the dream, you can regenerate if it hasn't quite come true yet. If you live for it, find it, and the dream is revealed as a nightmare, you die inside. I had to save myself.

So in October of 1962 I broke off with him, what proved to be the first of many breaks.

I felt relief when I had finished. I felt ballsy and euphoric. I felt so good that first night when I went out on the town by myself, free of him.

By 11:00 P.M. that night I was on the phone to Marc. When I couldn't reach him, I almost panicked. I called every twenty minutes from where I was until he finally answered the phone at 1:20 in the morning. I told him I loved him and couldn't live without him, that I could never say good-bye to him.

"Look, Rona," he said a bit hurriedly and without quite

as much feeling as I would have liked. "You know I'll never feel toward anyone like I feel toward you. We'll see each other tomorrow, O.K.?"

I could tell from his tone that he either had a girl with him or was on his way out to meet one. Dracula goes to bed late. It made me angry, hurt me again. But not enough. "Yes, tomorrow," I said.

I realized then why I had chosen this man, let him in when I had turned down all others, some of the biggest stars in the world, in fact, some of the most dashing young stars-to-be. I realized in that moment as I put the phone back into its cradle that the resolution and euphoria I felt earlier was the confidence of an addict who has just had her fix.

The drug had worn off.

It had taken about six hours.

I felt like I'd die without another dose.

Oh God in heaven, I'm as sick as he is!

I would stay as sick as he was for ten more years.

CHAPTER ELEVEN

As far back as 1959, I wondered about going on television. But now it was a *necessity*. It was the only way left to reach the top.

So I began *that* campaign. Every time I could save five hundred dollars, I hied myself off to New York to pound on the network doors.

Nothing. Nothing. *Nothing*.

I wasn't going to give up. I knew TV was the way. But I was hitting my head against a stone wall. Only it *couldn't* be a stone wall. There *had* to be a way in. I had what they needed.

It came to me on a Sunday afternoon in a Hollywood Olympic-sized pool.

We were talking about the latest Instant Superstar and how she had managed it.

"It's not just because she's got it, baby," someone said. "We *all* got it around this fuckin' pool. It's because she never does anything but *her* thing, every Goddamn time. She puts it all in one place. And boooom!"

I'm never going to try CBS and NBC again, I thought to myself in that instant.

ABC.

I decided to make them *my* "one place."

After years of going back and forth to New York whenever I could get up the money, sending them outlines, sending them story ideas, making a pilot that was rejected, I decided to drop everything except the television efforts.

Before I began writing, people in the know told me how "smart" I was to have changed my name to Barrett. "You'd never have made it in this business with Burstein," they said ominously.

When I started going around to the TV networks, I always noticed an air of unease—not at what I said, but at how I said it. I couldn't put my finger on it until one day, a second-in-command took me aside. "You'll never see yourself on national TV as long as there's a single trace of Brooklyn in your voice," he confided.

A trace of *Jew,* he meant.

I went to a speech teacher and "cured" it. It cost more money than I had. I wrote more stories. It didn't happen overnight. Sometimes the Brooklyn still emerges—it's really Queens, of course—and I'm damned proud of it. I'm not sure if *that* part isn't what allowed me to overcome all those bastards.

Because they *do* have to be overcome. There already was the "Jew quota" on the air waves, especially in news. "The only reason Rona Barrett's on TV is because she's having an affair with Elton Rule," I used to hear constantly once I'd broken in. The closest Elton and I ever came to having an affair was when he gave me a look for three seconds at the station Christmas party. Though he was a strong, strong man in business, it is really my opinion that Elton believed his penis would have fallen off if he ever put it in a Jewish girl. The same goes for just about every other high and mighty non-Jewish TV executive—except for those few who have a "thing" for going to bed with Jewish women (but never giving one an important show, unless they're simply dynamite entertainers like Dinah Shore or Barbra Streisand).

The anti-Semitism even filtered down to lower levels. So many clerical people in the ABC offices were disturbed at having a Jewish broad on the air that I began turning their own game against them. "I'm half Jewish and half Italian," I'd say. Then, like flies to the light, they'd all have to know which half was Jewish and which half was Italian! I even used to walk out of the office swearing in Italian when I just couldn't stand their shit anymore.

Not that anti-Semitism was new to me. During World War II, stars like Ward Bond and his friends were quite obviously not in the forefront of Zionism. To say the very least. I feel the Nixon Administration's assault on TV news coverage was actually an assault on the Jews who had pushed their way—and I'd be the first to admit, Jews *do* push—to the top of the three major networks.

But, you might wonder, how can there be so much anti-Semitism on TV if it's basically run by Jews? And the answer is sickeningly simple: In order to *maintain* their position, the paranoid Jewish executives are generally discriminatory against their own.

Not that *I'm* sitting in final judgment. Even the most ultraliberal Jews are usually guilty of prejudice in one form or another. I remember the day I caught Elliott Gould off guard, after asking him what he'd feel if his son someday brought home a black girl to marry. "I don't want to think about it!" was his automatic reaction. Once he thought about it, of course, he said it would be fine, just fi-iiii-ine.

As I write this, in fact, it occurs to me that *I* only had one Jewish lover—and that, too, was a disastrous affair. A couple of people have asked me why. I always said it was because I wasn't prejudiced against non-Jews, and that I had enough hang-ups of my own without getting involved with hung-up Jewish men. But could it also have been because I was—am—subconsciously prejudiced against my own?

Whatever, I sure as hell wasn't anti-anything when it came to work.

Debts I could pay by working nineteen hours a day instead of seventeen. A Brooklyn accent I could go to speech school for. But what about *being a woman?*

Being a woman.

It meant many things. First of all, it meant being the daughter of Harry and Ida Burstein. Through all my years in Hollywood, becoming more famous, making more money, they never stopped ending their Sunday long-distance calls to me with "Give up, Rona. Come home and be a secretary!"

There I was, however, pounding on network doors and getting no response. I had reached that point in my career where whatever I was doing seemed to be a detriment to my getting on TV. I hated being called the "Queen of the Fan Mags." The way press agents said it, I felt I was as close to being a whore. I quit writing for the magazines. And after writing five years for Bell-McClure and now making a big fat $100 a week and having my name appear in over 125 minor papers and realizing there was no way to make a nickel more, I decided to quit that, too. A number of people tried to convince me that I was being financially screwed by the syndicate and at one point I seemed to have enough proof that I was. But my lawyer advised me not to sue.

"You're not big enough," was his advice. "If you make trouble now another syndicate might think you're a troublemaker and no one wants a troublemaker in their stable. . . . Not propitious, Rona. Just take it as another lesson you've learned."

Bitterly and reluctantly, I took his advice. I never sued

the syndicate, but I did quit, much to Osenenko's regret.

I was now fully unemployed without the prospect of a job in sight. And as I have instinctively done in so many crucial hours I again put myself in a position where I could not run away. I did not want to hear my father say "Quitter!"

With a $2,000 settlement I received from an auto injury, I made a down payment on my first house. It was to be the first of five houses I remodeled, refurbished, and parlayed into the one where I'm living today. I didn't know it at the time, but my houses became my "secret lovers." With the completion of each remodeling it was time to move on to something bigger and better. I treated my homes like I should have treated the men in my life.

How I was going to pay for this first house was beyond my comprehension and my pocketbook.

Every Sunday my parents would call and beg me to give it all up and come home. One week my father would play the heavy and my mother would tell him to leave me alone. The next week my mother would nag and my father would tell her to get off my back. It was like being in the boxing ring against two heavyweights. Soon I felt absolutely beaten down. I wondered if they were right. Should I sell the house, go home, forget TV? Forget my *picture* . . . my *dream?*

I had thirty-six cents in the bank.

"All right," I said wearily to my mother that last Sunday. "I'll come home."

"No!" my father shouted suddenly. I was shocked at his tone. At his attitude. "I mean it, I really mean it. Don't quit. Just do me a favor." (As if I owed him one—but I listened.) "Just give it another twenty-four hours. I've got a good feeling," he said.

Twenty-four hours later, so help me God, I received

a phone call from KABC-TV. I had by now lost count of how many trips and how much money it had cost flying back and forth to New York trying to convince the ABC brass that I was right for their news operation. I had equally lost count of how many times I had traveled from my first apartment on Horn Avenue to Prospect and Talmadge to meet with the local KABC brass to convince *them* that they should at least test me in the Los Angeles market.

But Steve Mills, who was then the station's program manager, said Elton Rule, the vice-president and general manager, wanted to talk to me.

I don't remember the conversation but it boiled down to: Did I want to go on the 11:00 P.M. news with Baxter Ward?

Did I?!!

I wish to insert here that this generosity from ABC may have been prompted by a telegram I sent that Sunday night to Leonard Goldenson in New York. The telegram read: "After seven years of futzing around with me I would really like a decision. Do you or don't you want me? A simple yes or no will suffice."

The following day when Steve called, he was actually laughing.

"Leonard Goldenson wants to know what you mean by the word 'futzing.' I told him you probably mean 'fucking' but Western Union hadn't become that liberalized yet."

We both laughed.

One week later, on December 12, 1966, I made my TV debut. Some thirty of my friends gathered on my first kingsize bed, which I had purchased from the Nick Adamses, to watch me.

I was awful.

I was on film.

My feature story had been edited unmercifully.

I cried when my friends left.

My second night began with an exclusive interview with Tina Sinatra which really made waves. Even after I had to edit the hell out of it. To really understand what happened, I'll have to explain my entire relationship with the Sinatra family to you.

There is probably no entertainer nor any other family which rivals the Kennedys for having people all over the world ask about them than the Sinatras.

Jack Haley, Jr., at thirty-five, was a professional bachelor. He was always getting "engaged." To about forty-five different girls a year. It seemed as soon as some gal got to know the "real" Jack too well, she was off and running in the opposite direction. Or as soon as Jack felt some gal was getting hold of his scene, *he* flew the coop.

But with Nancy Sinatra it was different. Nancy, however, was adamant against getting married or engaged. First, she didn't want to be "another" of Jack's girls. Second, deep down she was a deathbed Catholic who could never quite come to grips with herself about premarital sexual relations.

Also, her divorce from Tommy Sands had nearly destroyed her. I never watched a human being suffer so deeply and so painfully as Nancy did when her marriage to Tommy ended. Tommy had packed his bag one day, walked into their bedroom and said, "Good-bye."

Nancy had said, "I'll see you later," thinking he was going down the hill to visit friends. Or maybe work.

"No," he said. "You don't understand. It's *good-bye,* Nanny. No later. I'm leaving. For good!"

Nancy fell apart.

Doctors were called in.

She became a living vegetable.

No one could communicate with her. She was like a pathetic baby, suffering from some disease for which there was no cure. I ached for her. But my heart also broke for Tommy. He was one of the kindest, most sensitive human beings I had ever known. Their marriage should never have happened—despite Nancy's devotion.

When Nancy was devoted, she was devoted all the way. She was to Tommy. After all, he had been her first lover. To her that was sacred. Tommy was *everything*.

He was her daddy reincarnated.

Therein lay the tragedy of the marriage.

All of Nancy's life she had looked for another Frank Sinatra to be her man. Anyone who has had the opportunity to see Nancy and Big Frank together, especially as she matured, would quietly walk away with a funny, gnawing feeling: *If they weren't father and daughter, they could certainly pass for lovers. . . .*

But Tommy Sands *wasn't* Frank Sinatra. He never could be. He was too sensitive, too raw, too sweet.

An old friend of theirs told me of an incident in Palm Springs during a weekend with Nancy and Tommy and a few other pals at Frank's house. This friend had been in the kitchen when Frank entered. He asked Frank, "Well, what do you think of your prospective son-in-law?"

Frank looked at him and said, "He's O.K. Too bad he doesn't have any balls, though."

Tommy Sands had balls.

It's simply that nobody has the balls Frank Sinatra has. When God gave out balls, Frank was definitely first in line!

So, in no way could Tommy Sands survive the siege of the Sinatras. From the moment Nancy and Tommy married in Las Vegas, he became a captive. Rarely was a decision made where the whole Sinatra clan didn't huddle so everyone could air his or her opinion.

I watched Tommy being swallowed up daily and wondered how long his sensitive soul could take it. And poor Nancy, she was truly innocent in those days! I'm sure she herself did not realize what she was doing, not only to her husband, but to herself. All she wanted for Tommy was success.

Success "like Daddy's!"

When Tommy begged her to let him do things on his own, Nancy would always acquiesce. But then she'd sneak around the corner, go to Daddy—or Daddy's friends—and ask for help. Like making sure Tommy got a part in a picture, a TV show, a better nightclub deal. I remember once he had to go to Nashville to record and couldn't afford to take Nancy with him. So she went and asked Frank for the private plane. Who knows what really kills a man's love?

That particular incident occurred the weekend prior to the kidnapping of Frankie, Jr., by the way. The call from the "kidnappers" came through as I was eating dinner with Mrs. Sinatra, Sr. "Good Lord, Rona," she whispered to me, holding one hand over the mouthpiece, "they've kidnapped Frank, Jr.!"

Although there isn't any hard evidence, in my heart of hearts I always felt Frank Jr. had staged his own kidnapping. Not for money. Not for publicity. But for the attention of his father. All his life he'd had to compete with Nancy for that—and he lost. I know there are people who disagree with me because some of the "criminals" are still in jail.

It was soon obvious to insiders that Tommy's love for
Nancy was slowly but surely dying. And that the unwit-
ting murderers were all the Sinatras. Nancy became nervous. She got painfully thin. In another effort to assert
himself, Tommy decided to throw away his singing career
and concentrate on becoming an actor. The Sands closed
their home in Hollywood and took a one-room apartment
on Lexington Avenue in New York where Tommy enrolled
in Lee Strasberg's Actor's Studio.

Nancy became more anxiety-ridden than ever. Something was definitely wrong, but she said nothing to any
of us. Under Strasberg's tutelage Tommy Sands became
a different human being. It was as if Tommy were going
through deep psychoanalysis. Strasberg ripped him of everything—his innermost fears and unspoken agonies. Then,
because of his own guilt feelings about what this was doing
to himself and to Nancy and to their marriage, Tommy
quit right in the middle of his studies! And there he stood,
naked, not knowing how to put his clothes back on.

He never was the same. His sudden departure came soon
afterward. It was inevitable—if Tommy as a human being
was to survive.

When Tommy walked out, it wasn't as unexpected as
Nancy had led her close friends to believe. She had pretended it would never happen. But pretending doesn't make
it so. She loved her first lover and under no circumstances
did she want a second one. Good Catholic girls only have
one lover, one husband. She simply couldn't afford to lose
Tommy!

With his leaving, she was no longer in control. The light
switch had finally turned off and, sadly, she could find

no way to turn it back on. Not even Daddy could help this time. None of his money or influence could bring Tommy Sands back. It took real balls for Tommy to walk out. And stay out. When Frank Sinatra wants you back because his daughter is an utter vegetable, you come back.

But Frank had even more balls than Tommy. He wasn't going to let Nancy suffer, no matter what.

After all else had failed, a psychiatrist finally convinced Nancy that the real reason Sands left was *not* because he didn't love her any more, but because he was totally incapable of loving *any* woman.

I think if someone had taken a knife and actually torn out Nancy's heart, it would have been less painful than what she felt upon hearing the psychiatrist's words. But something else *was* out, too—her love for Tommy.

Nancy Sinatra Sands got out of bed.

She no longer felt guilty over the failure of her marriage. *Tommy* was the failure!

Tommy's days now became a living nightmare. He eventually cracked up. I honestly cried off and on for a week when I saw him at Cedars of Lebanon Hospital.

As for Nancy, her head changed with that divorce. In trying to pull herself together, she found a career, a career she really no more wanted than she wanted a second nose. Yet it changed her, too. Her career gave her a sort of "I'll show you" attitude. I have always felt it was "I'll show you, Tommy Sands, what you really missed!"

And so when Nancy became engaged to Jack Haley, Jr., I reported it with a flip of the tongue. I felt once Nancy got to know Jack Haley, she would find he was only another watered-down version of Tommy Sands, and certainly no Frank Sinatra.

But, if history has any meaning, Haley had no intention of marrying Frank's daughter! When he got locked into the romance, he knew the only way out with a Sinatra was to make it look good. *Very* good. If he gave Nancy an engagement ring and they stayed engaged for a proper length of time, it would be okay if they then changed their minds. It would look a lot better to those chronicling Hollywood's—and Sinatra's—history.

And so, on a Wednesday night in early January, 1969, Jack Haley, Jr. slipped a diamond ring in the shape of a bee, clustered by another ring of diamonds, on Nancy's fourth finger, left hand. And Daddy magnanimously commented: "Anything that makes my Nancy happy makes me happy, too!"

But it did not make Nancy happy.

So it did not make Frank happy.

None of the Sinatras will ever by happy, no matter whom they marry, whom they control, what they accomplish.

They are, underneath their skin, the most unhappy family I have ever known.

They have everything the world can give. But they cannot give themselves relief from loneliness and frustration. That can only come from inside. And they don't have what it takes—for it takes even more than "balls."

I spent nearly eight years being what I thought was a close friend—"a third daughter" of the Sinatras, as Frank once put it. The demise of our friendship—yes, our *love*—came with dramatic and unexpected suddenness. It happened exactly two days after my debut on ABC-TV in December of 1966, the night I announced little Tina Sinatra's engagement to Sammy Hess. The family had consented to my interviewing Tina and Sammy on camera.

And the last thing in the world I wanted to do was hurt a Sinatra. I loved them.

In the middle of the interview, while asking Tina if she would be married in church by a priest or in temple by a rabbi (Hess is Jewish) Mrs. Sinatra interrupted, "I don't want you to ask that question. Cut it out!" she said loudly.

"Why?" I asked, shocked.

"I have my *private* reasons," she answered.

I promised her I could cut the "offending" question. Yet she interrupted several more times. Finally she decided it would be best if I asked Tina questions only about her upcoming career instead of the marriage. I did. I asked Tina innocuous questions like if she had any favorite actress she would like to emulate. I would have only done it for the Sinatras. "Oh, no one," she answered, by the way. "I'm told my beauty is so unique and my acting ability so fantastic, I won't remind anyone of anyone!"

When the tape was run on the news that night, Mrs. Sinatra called me screaming, raving and swearing. "Tina has never said any of those things!" she ranted. "You've dubbed her voice!"

I asked her how that could possibly be.

"It's someone else's voice on the track! All you're looking to do is use the Sinatra name to further your own career. You're like everyone else!" I guess in the end, that's what the Sinatras *must* feel about anyone. I had become too close. And now I was hurting like everyone else who truly liked that family and only enjoyed being their friend.

And the incident mushroomed. Nancy dropped me. She had been closer to me than my own sister. Why did *she* kill our friendship? "I'm tired of you being a dinner guest at my home and never sending me a thank you note," she ultimately told me. I couldn't believe it! Pfft! It was over like that. Eight years. Finished. Maybe I should have been thrilled. I remember somebody telling me, "The Sinatras only dump you when you become a somebody and they can't boss you around any more."

But even that wasn't the end. Though Mrs. Sinatra will not talk to me—and insists that none of the other Sinatras do—I know that she often watches me on TV. Mainly, I think, because she knows that through me she will always know what Frank's really up to.

That was Rona and the Sinatras. Still, if the Tina interview vaulted me closer to the pinnacle, it would all be worth it. In the last analysis, I wasn't on TV in order to be close to the stars. I was close to the stars so I could be on TV. Or *was* I? Sometimes it hurt me so much to lose a friend—let alone a whole family—that I wondered.

Either way, it didn't matter. After that one scoop, my show made absolutely no impact. One reason was that my boss Baxter Ward insisted on filming me instead of letting me do the show live. Then fate gave me a hand. The films kept getting fouled up in the soup can (the developing room) and I was receiving frantic telephone calls at eight or nine at night to haul my butt back to the station because I was going to have to go on live. It happened again and again. Toward the end of January 1967, the soup can fouled up my film one time too many. That night, after I had hurriedly returned to perform live, Baxter turned to me and in his shy, apologetic Southern way, said: "Do you think you could come here every night live? I don't want to trust the soup can anymore."

It was the greatest opportunity of my life.

Except that I was scared—shitless.

Literally. I had absolutely no saliva! My mouth became drier than sandpaper. When the floor manager got the signal from the director I felt like I was walking the stairs to the Manhattan subway again.

I totally panicked whenever I saw that red light go on. *Live.*

What I *was*—anything I said—would without one iota of editing go into millions of homes. . . . But that's how my career on TV really began. Things started looking way up.

Until—again—I received a stab in the back from fate.

ABC planned a new network half-hour magazine show about Hollywood. It was the show *I* had submitted to them. Only now it was to have a different title, produced by a man I had never heard of, starring an actress, Joanna Barnes, who was anything but a journalist. Out of the incredible kindness of their hearts, however, the producers of *my* show asked me if I'd like to do a tiny segment on the show giving the Hollywood news.

"I want to sue!" I told my lawyers. They wouldn't let me.

I was as bitter as I've ever been. But I accepted their meager offer, never letting any one of them forget they were thieves. Someday I'd find a way to get even.

As I had known from the beginning, actresses have a talent for acting, not interviewing. Joanna was a beautiful girl, but she was more interested in how she looked than in the questions she was asking.

Her interviews bombed while my news segments, quite frankly, were saving the show. With thirteen shows to be completed, Joanna and ABC came to a parting, and I was given the job of replacing her, though at *no* extra money.

"This is your opportunity," said Len Goldberg, then the head of ABC's daytime programming.

And I did make it my opportunity. Without any help from the powerful press division at ABC, the rating on "Dateline Hollywood" began to climb.

But it was too late. The show had already been cancelled and something else bought to replace it.

CHAPTER TWELVE

When "Dateline" died, I was lucky. I did not. I still had my news reports with Baxter, and more than ever it became important to be known as something more than just a "gossip columnist."

I began by scooping the competition time and again. Like the Elvis Presley exclusive:

Unless the world turns upside-down, Elvis Presley will marry his long-time girlfriend, Priscilla Bealieu, in Palm Springs this weekend. We have it on reliable authority that Priscilla's parents are already flying in from Northern California to attend the ceremony . . . as is Elvis' Dad from Memphis, Tennessee, and several other close friends and relatives. We hope this scoop doesn't spoil Elvis' plans.

That was the story. It really "made" me. Only there was more. Much more.

First, not since the days of Rudolph Valentino had any star had greater supporters than "the Pretzel." I therefore conclude that there must be something special about a guy so many millions find so worthy of adoring.

But for the life of me, I can't figure out what.

My relationship with Elvis is important in my life for two reasons. First, it's a good example of how I like to

track down a story. Second, I go back to the very beginning
of Elvis' rise to stardom, yet I honestly admit I know
next to nothing about him. He is the epitome of the unholy
marriage of media cowardice and personal no-risking.

I was one of the first teenage reporters to interview
Elvis. I owed that to Nick Adams, who had the most
fantastic nose in the world for smelling superstar material.

Maybe because Nick wanted so badly to be a superstar
himself.

Nick adored Elvis. Yet to this day, I feel that the Pelvis
is only the incarnate imagination of his mentor genius,
Colonel Tom Parker; that if one were to really stick a
pin in El, he'd go up in smoke!

The Colonel was afraid to let anyone who really knew
the alphabet, get to the kid. Talk about controlled news!
The lone intelligent columnist who ever got to interview
Elvis was Hedda Hopper. How? Only after she cleverly
wrote tons of negative things about him so that the Colonel was forced into it. However, by the time she got to
talk to him, even Hedda had been so brainwashed about
what a nice, sweet, intelligent lad he was that the interview
came out almost like all the others!

No Hollywood star hides behind a greater cloak of media
security than Elvis. In the amazing twenty years he has
been on the market, I have never seen or known him to
wander out alone. He is always surrounded by his "Memphis Mafia." Many years ago, before he really settled here,
I once got up to Elvis' suite at the Beverly-Wilshire Hotel.
He was dating Juliet Prowse at the time and one of his
regular little evening parties had been planned. A slew
of Hollywood gals had been invited to the hotel. I had
to swear on a *Bible* that I wouldn't come as Rona Barrett,

but as Susie Q. I got in because one of his boys at that time had a slight yen for me.

I can only tell you I'm glad that the walls at the Beverly-Wilshire are thick.

Public fornicating has just never been my style.

I think it took a lot of girls a lot of guts to date Elvis. I imagine Elvis could do well living in a Kibbutz. Then again, I'm told his Graceland home in Memphis, is almost like one. Not to mention the one in Trousdale. And the latest one. I must say that night was an experience even I shall never forget.

Nor shall I ever forget, that with the beginning of Elvis, began the true teenage sexual revolution in America which eventually spread through the whole world. Elvis spoke their language. He expressed a new sense of freedom we teenagers had been searching for. He threw away the keys to our chastity belts and the world went crazy.

By 1960, there were forty million more young people in America between the ages of thirteen and thirty than had ever existed before. The Clark Gables and Jimmy Stewarts were definitely now of another era and another age. They already had been captured and chronicled in print by Louella, Hedda, Sheila, and Kilgallen.

And so, on April 27, 1967, it was a strange thrill for me to learn from an unimpeachable but unrevealable source that Elvis Presley was at long last going to give up his anti-establishment status and marry Priscilla Beaulieu, the little gal he had met while he had been stationed in Germany during the Korean conflict! She had been fourteen at the time.

By the time I reported this, got off the air, and hightailed it to Palm Springs, AP and UP (who rarely like to admit they monitor my broadcasts daily), put out one of their "own" wire stories on Elvis' impending marriage. And so, by the time I arrived in Palm Springs, there were hordes of cameramen and photographers staked out all around Elvis' rented $750,000 home!

I needed an ally. So I joined forces with Tony Bowen, a magazine writer and a good guy. We knew immediately that with all those cameramen and reporters around, Elvis wouldn't do a bloody thing in broad daylight. We decided to stake out the town instead.

First, we discovered all of Priscilla's family registered at the Ramada Inn, just down the block. I made a few calls to some sources I had in town and soon learned that a group of them had been hired to go to Elvis' house on Saturday night for a "private party." We then staked out the house for a few hours to see who was coming and going. Through one of the open windows, we spied Elvis' dad. In the next several hours, all kinds of strange people came and went.

I sent Tony back to the Ramada Inn to check on the Bealieus. He trapped a few of them by the pool, but they refused to say anything.

Tony and I then decided to see the key florists. We first picked one near Elvis' home, and Tony went inside, pretending he was one of Elvis' boys, wanting "to check on the flowers." Fortunately, we chose the right one to begin with. *The man had a huge order for Elvis.* As cover, Tony ordered another arrangement to be included!

We went back to the house. It was getting dark. Everyone inside whom we could see from the open windows was still dressed casually. We spied a maid leaving a side door and followed her. She headed toward a market where we cornered her. She laughed and giggled and said she knew nothing, except that she'd run out of coffee and milk.

Sunday morning eventually came around and a lot of reporters decided to leave. The "private party" had *been* a private party.

Could my scoop have been a bust?

Tony and I didn't give up.

Yet all day Sunday, nothing happened. Something had gone wrong—drastically wrong. I began to feel that they had changed their plans because of my story!

It was late Sunday afternoon when Joe Esposito, one of Elvis' long-time business associates, appeared.

He got into his car.

I followed him.

He stopped at the market.

I trapped him.

He couldn't help but smile, said, "We all nearly fell off our chairs Thursday night when you announced the marriage. Who leaked a lie like that to you?"

Joe really tried to throw me off the track. In front of the soup counter, too. I told him he was a liar, that if the wedding wasn't going to take place, how could he explain the following five facts? (1) If Elvis wasn't getting married, how come a hundred dress shirts were delivered to his room at the Beverly-Wilshire Hotel before he was taken to Palm Springs? And ninety-nine were returned. (2) How come his Memphis jeweler arrived in Los Angeles carrying two wedding rings in his knapsack? (3) What was Elvis' best friend, George Kline, the busy DJ from Memphis, doing in Palm Springs "just for 48 hours"? (4) The florist. (5) What were all the Bealieus doing at the Ramada Inn, with one Bealieu woman after another getting her hair spruced up at the beauty parlor?

I told Esposito I could go on and on. Joe stared at me for a minute and succumbed. "Please don't ask me anything else, Rona. I don't want to lie to you. O.K.?"

But when *was* the wedding going to take place? Tony and I put our heads together, figured out the Colonel was probably masterminding the whole event. He'd flip if any one reporter got a beat on another reporter. Thus the wedding would take place at the precise time when it would be "all for one, one for all." But *when?*

Two hours later, a message was sent to me that Danny Kaye—also in for the festivities—was warming up his Lear Jet for an early morning ride to Las Vegas.

I headed for the airport.

At the ungodly hour of 2:30 A.M., Elvis and the group sneaked out of the house, were whisked to the airport and flew to Las Vegas in Danny Kaye's plane. At an even more ungodly hour of 5:30 A.M., Elvis Presley married Priscilla Bealieu with a wedding breakfast taking place at around 7:30 A.M., at the Stardust Hotel.

The details of the Elvis story weren't crucial. What *was* crucial was the control of news involved. Maybe it was mere "celeb gossip," maybe I wanted to think I was important in the bigger scheme of things, but I honestly felt like a crusader there in Memphis, breaking through their almost fascist secrecy.

Elvis Presley has a right to get married privately like anyone else, right? I agree. If—and it's a big if—he doesn't use the media night and day to fill all his other needs. Needs he knows that, if filled, will make a secret wedding a contradiction in terms. And they *were* filled, as with few other performers. You cannot have it both ways. If Elvis Presley wanted to be a truly private person, he should have become something less conspicuous.

The Dyan Cannon-Cary Grant divorce was another of my big scoops. That was how I got to be called "Miss Rona."

Even my own anchorman, Baxter Ward, had doubted my authority on that one. It wasn't until three days after I had broken the story that it made national headlines. Then Baxter began to develop some faith in me. I watched his sardonic manner change the night he held up the *Los Angeles Times* with the headlines I had announced three nights before. He absolutely melted and said, "Let's listen to the authority—our Miss Rona." With his Southern background, the greatest compliment he could pay a lady to show his respect was to call her Miss.

The name stuck.

And it began to mean something important.

On April 23, 1969, my lead item was: "Connie Stevens learned today that she was being divorced by Eddie Fisher—while watching a news program on Las Vegas TV. She was shocked!"

I used those twenty-four words because I couldn't use most of the rest you'll read now.

First, the divorce itself didn't mean much to anyone except the two little babies produced by the "ha-ha happy couple." I had predicted it a year before. Eddie told me at that time that he couldn't stand Connie, didn't know how he got himself into another marital mess, except that they had an incomparable sex life together.

The little Jewish boy from Philadelphia is a boob, of course. He was never very bright and, emotionally speaking, he wasn't even ready for his bar mitzvah at thirty! I think the thing I began to dislike most about Eddie, of course, was that he wished he hadn't been born a Jew.

Many years have passed and Eddie has gone through

several non-Jewish marriages since I had my ups and downs with him. It was during one of these ups that I became privy to Eddie's knowledge of Connie Stevens.

I learned that Connie was pregnant with Eddie's child and that they were not married. I remained silent about the subject. Knowing Eddie's background, I was quite sure that he and Connie would marry. However, as the months progressed and her condition became more and more obvious, I realized Hollywood would soon be faced with a present-day Ingrid Bergman-Rossellini affair.

Eddie Fisher was at the Waldorf-Astoria. My sources in New York kept reporting to me that he had kept reporting to them that he would *not* marry Connie—no matter what. If she wanted to have his child, that was perfectly O.K. with him.

I placed a call to Eddie at the Waldorf. I asked him straight out if he was going to marry Connie. He replied, "No." In the ninth month of Connie's pregnancy, with some people saying they were secretly married, some arguing that they weren't, and still others asserting it wasn't Eddie's baby at all, I broke the story and set things straight. Of course, the pregnancy story was a scoop only to the general public who had never viewed Connie's tummy.

I spent nearly two hours writing that fourteen-second story. I knew this was the kind of story that would have its effect on everyone involved. I knew I would make enemies. It would make Eddie come off a heel. My job is sometimes not a pretty one. I have no rules except my own conscience. I'm not always right.

Several months after Connie had given birth, the rumors took a new turn—that Eddie was going to kick Connie out of his house as soon as she and the baby could be "relocated." It was again during another "up" period with Eddie that I learned this. Despite my breaking the story of Connie's pregnancy, Warren Cowan, Eddie's public relations man, had brought us back together. Eddie's bad press ever since he botched the Elizabeth Taylor marriage had left him with an "image problem." Warren thought that if Eddie leveled with me, perhaps I would be the old good friend I used to be. I was willing to try, though I must admit I had my doubts. Eddie was still Eddie.

A few days later, he rang my doorbell. He had a terrible toothache. As I recall, a cap had fallen off his tooth, and Eddie had left a message with his answering service for his dentist to call him. We began talking about *Paint Your Wagon* which, at that time, he was going to produce, also, his meetings with Kim Novak about a property he had bought while still married to Elizabeth Taylor, in which Liz was to have starred. Other career stuff.

Then, out of the blue, Eddie said, "Why don't you report on TV about my secret meetings with Kim for *off*-the-screen reasons?"

"But what about Connie?"

"I couldn't care less about her," Eddie sneered. He went on to tell me that he didn't know how in the world he had gotten himself into this mess. "She's a bore," he said. "I can't stand her friends, either. She drives me crazy, but she's the best fuck I ever had!" He went into detail then.

I felt myself blushing. I was accustomed to hearing celebrities talk intimately, but coming from Eddie it struck me as strange and vulgar. I wondered: *If Connie was such a great mistress, where did that leave Liz Taylor?* Liz's conversion to Judaism must have ruined everything. Eddie then went on and on for what seemed hours, telling me how much he couldn't stand Connie. She was a slob. She didn't keep the house clean. He didn't like her "Gumbah" friends. He didn't like her father. He didn't like her mother. He didn't like her interfering with his friends.

A few days later I reported, at Eddie's request, the story about Kim Novak. All hell broke loose at his house. Connie was up in arms!

Eddie had previously told her *she* would be the star of the picture, it turned out.

Soon after, I remembered reading in everyone else's columns about the TV columnist who had been going around maliciously making up stories about Connie and Eddie, who actually were secretly married.

Well, Eddie and Connie *did* secretly marry. In the Caribbean in 1968.

After she became pregnant with their second baby.

To this day, I have not been able to get some of the details of the Eddie-Connie relationship published. In a supposedly grown-up America, this seems incredible. Yet I was learning the hard way that the liberated clothes our country has put on are *only* a put-on.

But there were more important things.

One of them was seeing the truth break through—and my struggle to break through to the pinnacle with it.

Why were all the American media geared to half-truth? Could it be because, beneath it all, the public wanted it that way? That they were able to take a vague, fictional glimpse of the truth on the TV or video screen, and then only if they could go home saying, "It's only a story."

Very few people want to put in that kind of effort. Part of their cop-out is not facing the same thing in the heroes and leaders who represent them.

Well, I was going to *make* them face it. No matter how

they hamstrung me, no matter what they had against me, they had to keep me.

Because I raised the Nielsen television ratings for . . .

I raised the ratings by coming up with so many scoops that most of them got through by sheer force of numbers.

Like Darryl Zanuck is ready to kick his son Richard out as head of 20th Century Fox. I continued that saga with such accuracy I was told Darryl threatened to get ABC to fire me. He allegedly accused me of affecting 20th's stock—it kept going down. Leonard Goldenson refused to listen even if 20th threatened to pull all their TV material from ABC. I reported the news within the confines of fair doctrine — if Zanuck wanted to sue, he could ! He didn't. And in the final analysis, everything I ever said became a reality.

And there was the reported Lauren Bacall — Eric Sevareid two some. And now Sevareid was threatening to sue . He'd recently married. Our man Martin in London had seen Sevareid and Bacall in Paris . . . I did a follow-up item getting Sevareid off the hook. He thanked me. . . .

And then there were some Hubert Humphrey stories . . . rather bawdy . . . and the secret to Mae West looking so young. She took a low colonic, daily. Her press agent, Stan Musgrove, one May Day sent me a 45¢ enema bag with a note: "Stay pretty. Love, Mae."

Being a woman, of course, mainly meant being a woman among men in a man's world. All my life I'd fought male chauvinism in one form or another, but I never saw it so blatantly, sickeningly displayed as when I finally tried to reach the top of the man's world. I could fill a second book with the details. Let's simply try one on for size: My contract was unique. It was for fifty-two weeks— *without any vacation*. Today that would be illegal. Maybe then, too. But it was take it or leave it.

Still, I *was* getting paid the big money people make when they're on national television.

I *was?* With ABC, I was paid *local* rates—as if I were on one hometown station instead of the five biggest markets in the country. And when I voluntarily left ABC for the improved Metromedia deal, it was a *woman,* a "friend," who spent almost as much energy telling people I was fired as she spends promoting her books.

Most of all, though, being a woman meant simply . . . being a woman.

When you come right down to it, thirty million people reading you or watching you is merely another form of being loved. Or, at the very least, of getting attention. Yet there's no true substitute for the love of one man for a woman.

I needed *that.* By 1969, I was really making waves on TV. I had started on KABC but after less than a year and a half, I was reluctantly added to the news in ABC's five owned and operated stations. My show was covering 40 per cent of the country. The $600 a week I was earning had to pay staff and legmen and so forth, so I only took home about $200. I asked for a raise and they refused, even though they were getting all kinds of telephone calls and letters from affiliates who wanted me on their stations. In the middle of it all, *Life* came out with a five-page center spread on me. I knew I was hot. I knew I had to make the most of this opportunity or I'd be a goner. I asked for a raise. I asked to go on the full network or at least be distributed on the DEF (delayed electronic feed—like a wire service). The National Association of Broadcasters convention was taking place in Washington. A member of the affiliates' board of governors proposed to Elmer Lower, the president of ABC news, that he put me on the network or at least allow the affiliates to pick me up on the DEF.

Lower allegedly answered, "As long as I'm president of this news that will never happen. I don't believe what Rona Barrett does is news or newsworthy." Off the record, it was reported to me that he said, "I'd rather drop dead than have Rona Barrett on my news."

The same member turned to Elton Rule, who by this time had been made president of the network. My dear Elton turned up his palms to the heavens and said, "Gentlemen, it's true. Rona has helped raise the rating on all our stations, but I have nothing to do with the news. I suggest you contact Miss Barrett personally."

Within five minutes of that conversation a phone call was made to me in Los Angeles. I knew then that if I remained with ABC I would always be the little kid in the stock room. I would never get a fair shake. I had to move. I had to get out of my contract.

I called my lawyer, and asked him to get me out. It took me nearly three weeks to extricate myself from my new contract which I had signed only months before. Half a dozen execs at ABC did not want me to leave, the other half said "Good riddance."

It was Leonard Goldenson who finally sent word to the president of the owned and operated stations to give me an unconditional release.

The president was a man named John Campbell, whom I detested, and not only because he didn't like me. When he became the manager of KABC after Rule became network president, all Campbell seemed to do was destroy everything Rule had made good. He needled Baxter, challenged his autonomy, let me know he thought it was a mistake for me to be on television anywhere but Hollywood. In the end he made it simple for Baxter to leave to run for mayor of L.A., and he made it simple for me to quit. Eventually sportscaster Jim Healy was the only one left, and he quit too. In a matter of a few short months KABC's news rating was back in the toilet and Campbell was kicked upstairs and made president of the owned and operated stations. He was short-lived in that job, too.

Several months later, Freddie Fields of CMA told me how my release really came about. He was in a meeting with Goldenson and had brought my name up. Goldenson said he didn't want to let me go. He thought I added something different to the news and it certainly was an attention-getter. Freddie allegedly said, "But, Leonard, are you willing to fight Elmer and put her on the full network?"

Leonard allegedly replied, "I can't right now, Freddie."

"Then you should let her go. She's got an opportunity to go bigger. Give her a chance."

Leonard did. When Freddie told me the story, I sent Leonard a note that simply said, "Thank you." I hope he now understands why I did it.

One week after my release I was on Metromedia Television. Prior to my leaving ABC my lawyer had inquired that if he could get me free was Metromedia interested? Dick Woollen, head of programming, said yes.

My first week on Metromedia, I not only had pretty much the same markets as I had with ABC, but I had an additional seventeen markets around the country. Despite the heavy negative reaction from news directors, who felt much like Elmer Lower, I managed to get over fifty markets in the five years I've been on Metromedia. It should be over a hundred. But nothing has ever come easy to me.

I became the unchallenged leader in my field. When Johnny Carson wanted somebody to pick on, he picked on me. The "Rona Barrett doesn't have to cut her steak with a knife" remark came one night after I ran the scoop item on his divorce-to-be. John *was* mad then, but the truth is that all the knocks he's put on me since (and me on him) are just the two of us knocking what's good for each other. When we meet in person, I like him very much and he always gives me a big, sincere kiss. On the mouth.

Not that I left my career to chance once I was on TV. It was great to have Johnny Carson promoting me, but very frankly, I don't think I took a back seat to anyone except Jackie Susann in promoting myself. Every week I did about a dozen major things to reach the people who didn't watch the show—like sending out transcripts of the entire broadcast to five dozen key people—and literally hundreds of minor things.

Partly it was ambition.

Partly it was escape from the pain.

It was hard to keep friends and even harder to do without. If I wrote the truth about them, they stopped being friends. If I tried to conceal the truth, it was a painful full-time job. Nick Adams was one such job.

To begin the story of Nick Adams, let's back up a couple of years. It was Vaughn Meader's opening night at the Crescendo nightclub. Nick was asked to send out the invitations and to be the master of ceremonies. Nick was not the greatest for holding his liquor, but if he got past two drinks without falling asleep, one could expect *any-*

thing. As producer Mervyn LeRoy said to me when I asked him why he invited Nick to all his parties: "Because he makes people laugh!" And in the jungle of Hollywood, that's almost as good as having thirty million smackers in the bank.

Anyway, on this particular evening, I had just returned from a trip to New York, where I had again worn out a pair of shoes and boots trying to convince the TV networks to transform my newspaper column into a newspaper column of the air. I was not in the best of spirits, but the then owner of the now defunct Crescendo (Shelly Davis, a producer, and perhaps my closest male friend) insisted I go to the opening. He also wanted me to meet the new *Life* bureau chief, a young, attractive guy. I went.

Nick *had* made it past the two drinks. When the time came to begin Vaughn Meader's introduction, Nick started introducing every mother, aunt, uncle, and star in the room. The introductions went on for more than forty minutes and they were getting funnier and funnier. Nick was surpassing himself. I thought to myself: I can't imagine how Meader will be able to follow this.

Finally, Nick got around to introducing Vaughn. There was a sigh of relief from the audience, including Shelly, the bureau chief, and myself. However, it was strange that sitting ringside was a girl Nick was going to marry at one time, and whom he had *not* introduced—actress Kathy Nolan, seated with her new bridegroom. Kathy was about the only one Nick hadn't mentioned.

No sooner had the thought crossed my mind when, in the midst of his Meader intro, Nick stopped short and screamed: "Oh, my God! I forgot to introduce the greatest broad I've ever known in my whole life. . . . The only broad I know who's as good out of the sack as in the sack . . . the greatest lay . . . the best broad . . . a super broad . . . in and out of the sack . . ."

You could have heard an option drop in the stupefied audience.

I whispered to Shelly: "Omigod, he's talking about Kathy! He forgot to introduce her, and she's sitting there with her new old man!"

Shelly whispered back: "Can't believe his bad taste. Can't *believe* it. He just *can't* do it!"

The bureau chief could only look back and forth at the two of us.

Nick suddenly paused.

A dawning sanity came into his eyes.

He took a deep breath, looked around the room. What would he do?

From what seemed like a great distance a voice penetrated. It was Nick's. I heard him saying: "Ah . . . ah . . . I mean our next Louella and Hedda rolled into one . . . RONA BARRETT!!!"

There was a gasp from the audience. Like a giant vacuum cleaner. Everyone's head turned toward my booth.

I started to laugh—like a jet blast—and I couldn't stop.

It rippled across the room, erupted into a volcano as others began to laugh with me. The tremendous tidal wave of laughter sounded like a ludicrous giant audience tape . . . laughing . . . laughing till tears were rolling down faces and people in rag doll poses were rolling in their chairs.

Eventually, in the wake of the noses being blown, subsiding groans, moans and rebursting of chuckles, the bureau chief leaned toward me.

"How about a date Thursday night?" he asked.

I had never been to bed with Nick Adams.

But I looked at Kathy Nolan with open admiration!

That was the Nick Adams I knew and loved. But the years took a sad toll on him, and the rest of the story picks up several years later, when I was established on ABC.

I had several parties to attend that night. Mainly, a bash being given at the $400,000 Trousdale mansion of Irv Levin and his then wife Lenny. Levin was then the head of production for the National General Corporation, soon to be president of NGC. Their party was in honor of Carol White, a poor woman's Julie Christie.

It was no different than a lot of other Hollywood parties except that it was held in a little nicer home and the Levins were a little nicer kind of people. Irv wouldn't know how to be phony if you gave him a twenty-year Hollywood course in it. Not many of the press were invited, but there were a lot of "heavy-type" industry names.

Bob Marcucci, my other best friend, escorted me. We giggled privately at all the bullshit being thrown around. Sometimes, to be frank, I enjoyed playing the game and I got so good at it that I could pass "GO" one hundred times and collect dozens of two-hundred-dollar items in just a couple of hours. That was my mood on that evening.

Little did I know that right down the street from the party, over a short hill, one of my few intimate friends had taken his last breath.

ABC had frantically tried to reach me but, ironically, I'd failed to check in with my service that one night. While I'd been partying, my poor, tormented Nick had been found dead in his home. His fully clothed body was found propped up against his bed.

To this day there are still several questions as to what really happened. Such as:

Whatever happened to the huge chain of keys Nick always carried with him?

How did he get into his house without them?

What happened to the suitcase he eccentrically kept filled with small bills?

What became of the address book he always carried with him?

Most of all: Was it really the gutsy Nick style to take an overdose of anything to end it all? I'm afraid that, finally, it was.

The year preceding Nick's untimely death had been a nightmare for him and those who were close to him. I was perhaps the only person who knew how remorseful Nick was for what he had done. He had committed the sickest act of his entire life and obviously found it difficult in the end to accept himself any longer. I believe this tender, tragic human being hated himself as few people have hated themselves.

One week before he died he had paid me a visit. The doorbell rang at around 8:00 in the morning. When I opened the door, I scarcely recognized him. He looked so tired, thin, different. He asked me for a cup of coffee. I knew he was asking for much more.

Nick poured his heart out that morning. He kept saying over and over again, "I love her, Rona. Why did I do it to her? I love her . . . *they* made me . . . they *made* me!"

Nick had filed for custody of his children during that dreadful year. His marriage to Carol Nugent had gone sour. They were that rare, pitiful couple who can't live with *or* without each other. They had two kids, Allyson and Jeb, who worshipped them both.

Yet when Nick's rather successful series, "The Rebel,"

was over, it seemed as though a crucial part of his existence
was over, too. All his life he only had one dream: to be
a superstar and build an empire. "You and me, baby! We're
gonna have the biggest fuckin' empire this town ever heard
of. You and me, baby," he'd say. "We'll own this fuckin'
town!" I'd heard his crude expression so many times in
the fifteen years I knew Nick that I often saucily threatened to make a recording of it as my Christmas gift to
him.

The empire never came into being.

And the superstar star never quite was hung on his
dressing room door.

Nick couldn't take it. Whatever his beautiful qualities,
he refused to recognize his faults and work with them.
He was always placing the blame on others. He began
to drink heavily. He was always a drinker, but in the last
years, he became what can only be termed an alcoholic.
He couldn't seem to make it through the day or the night
without a six pack of beer down his gut, followed by
stronger stuff.

Worst of all, he began blaming his failures on Carol.
During one of his crazed states he remarked to me—and
to a whole roomful of people—that he wasn't making it
because no one in Hollywood's upper stratosphere would
accept his wife. He referred to her as a "plain Jane" who
didn't know how to entertain properly, couldn't carry on
a conversation and, in general, was totally incapable of
being with important people.

This was untrue. She was one of the most refreshing
Hollywood wives in the entire community. However, Carol
didn't know how to lie. She was no phony.

Nick had learned how to lie.

Especially to himself.

It was too difficult for him to admit, as it is with so many people, that he was insecure. And so he would blanket this by being loud and obnoxious and always "on." It became almost unbearable for Carol to go out in public with Nick. At some time during the evening he always embarrassed himself and her and a lot of other people who were within earshot.

Nick accused Carol, in the courts of Los Angeles, of being an unfit mother because of indiscreet affairs she had in front of her kids. Carol was never indiscreet, though she was up-front. And he never once mentioned his own affairs. Nick was almost always on the make, trying to prove he was a master lover.

To prove he was a manly man, he often publicly opened his fly and threatened to expose himself. In his last years, he seemed to get a great charge from walking around his house in the nude and even answering the doorbell *au naturel.*

What was behind it all? The core answer is the same one which tipped the scale toward disaster for so many men in Hollywood.

Nick had become the companion to a group of salacious homosexuals.

Fags can be as evil as straights, and this group enjoyed catering to his neuroses, loved telling him he *was* a superstar. They were like vampires who got their kicks sapping the goodness of his soul. They fed him back with their own poisons. He sat in my home so many times, trying to convince me that I had been fooled by Carol as he had been fooled.

Carol was rotten.

Carol was evil.

Carol was the real reason he was a failure.

Carol was . . . *woman?*

He had to "destroy Carol before she destroys me." He almost succeeded. But in so doing he destroyed himself. Literally.

When at the eleventh hour he focused back into reality to make amends, it was too late. Carol had been crucified. There was no unnailing her from the cross. All he could do was nail himself to it with her.

It was at 8:00 that morning (almost one year after publicly announcing on TV that he was divorcing Carol, while she sat at home unaware of his plans) that Nick cried his eyes out to me. He swore that Carol and the kids were the only people who meant anything to him and that he had "fucked up" their lives. Now he didn't know what to do about it. He asked me if I thought Carol could ever forgive him.

And then he cried some more.

I had never seen a man's spirit openly broken before. Most of all a friend's spirit.

But I had no words of comfort for Nick that morning. I just let him talk and cry.

He got up finally, left. He hugged me tightly first. I kissed him. "Today is a bad one, Nick," I whispered. "I just know tomorrow will be better."

One week later my friend was dead. A bottle of hydramedaphine was found empty on his dresser. The coroner's report said Nick Adams died from too much hydramedaphine in his system.

To hell with coroners. Nick Adams was dead. A collage painting which he had done for me a month before he died was hanging in my bedroom. I cried myself to sleep.

CHAPTER THIRTEEN

At the beginning of our relationship, I asked Marc why he had never been married. After all, he was over thirty in a town when three marriages by that age weren't uncommon. He gave a long dissertation which seemed extremely honest and vulnerable and revealing.

After we had been an "item," as they say, for a while, he took me up to his family's cabin in the mountains for a weekend. Much to his surprise, his mother and sister had decided to use the cabin too that Saturday and Sunday. We had to make the best of it. For me, it turned out the worst.

I was sitting with his sister on the end of the pier that led from their house down to the lake. We were dangling our legs in the water like two schoolgirls, watching Marc water-ski.

"Your brother certainly has a beautiful body," I finally said to her.

"Yeah, he's broken a lot of hearts," she replied. Then: "Have you ever seen his son?"

! ! !

I had never even *heard* of any son. It took me several deep breaths before I could question her. The story went like this: Marc had gotten a girl pregnant seven years ago and had married her just to give the kid a name. As soon as his son was born, Marc took off. He never saw either the child or the wife again. His mother and sister saw them both frequently, but *he* wouldn't have anything to do with his son.

My first reaction was agony. Utter agony. He'd done to this poor, innocent child he had created just what he was doing to me.

Yet a few seconds later, I felt ecstasy!

Ecstasy at the hope that he would marry me too one day.

After all, if he had done it once, he might do it again. No, I would never use the pregnancy routine on him. But still, the fact that he'd married once—no matter on what terms—gave me a crazy hope for our own future.

Yet, Marc continually proved that he couldn't make that kind of commitment to another human being. Time and again I opened up with him, tried to break through his wall by telling him things about myself, feelings I had, that I hadn't revealed to anybody before. Yet I couldn't go past a certain point—because he wouldn't let me. All he'd have to do was to give me a *look* and I knew that if I said another word . . .

And yet, frantically as he wanted to avoid any commitment, whenever he was in danger of losing the possibility of it completely, he would pursue me like a madman! In those rare moments, he was more tender than a father to a new baby. *My God, he is changing,* I began saying to myself. *He's really wonderful. I always knew it!*

Marc was like an incredibly endowed athlete who keeps tying the game up in the last of the ninth.

But never wants to win it.

Of course, Marc wasn't there to be tender at many of my most crucial moments. Inevitably, even when we were apart, I would gravitate to people who knew him. And they would regale me with some of the most moving compliments I had ever been paid.

From Marc.

Them he could tell.

Me he *couldn't.*

It kept me coming back. *That's what he really feels,* I'd think. I'd always come back to my father for the same reason. Daddy would say even better things about me to others than my mother. But before I left for California, all he could tell me was, "You'll never make it as a writer. Who do you think you are? You're just an ordinary kid who has ordinary parents. Be safe. Stay with us."

I'll never forget my father's words. They only made me more determined than ever to prove he was wrong. Everyone was wrong. Anybody could become somebody if they believed, and I had begun to become a writer. I don't mean merely feature stories about stars or gossip columns. I had begun *The Lovomaniacs,* which would be a bestseller, was developing two ideas for screenplays which I wanted to produce and direct myself, and I had written 150 pages of my own life story.

Fictionalized.

I called myself Moira.

I couldn't yet face Rona.

But I *was* becoming a writer and a damned good one at times. My father was wrong. Just as Marc was wrong in not being able to say to me, give to me, *to me,* what he could say *about* me, give to me through *others.*

I knew why.

Beneath it all, he didn't believe *he* would make it.

I could never get all the way into him to find out what his real dream was. I only knew that he didn't dare to dream it openly.

I had. No matter what manure I've covered my life and my psyche with, in one way I'd stayed pure. I'd dared to dream and I'd dared to be naked about those dreams.

About being at the top.

And about being at the top with one man.

I wasn't going for a tie.

In 1965, things got uglier with Marc than ever before. It was no longer enough for him to make it with every girl in town. Now he was making it with all my girl friends.

I remember one night in particular. We'd had an especially bad time of it three days before, hadn't talked until that morning. Then, in a rare moment of tenderness, he said he'd like to have dinner at my house.

The time was 8:30. I prepared a special feast, trying to make everything right one more time, for the thousandth time.

He usually arrived late. This time he was twenty minutes early. I began to feel that old uncontrollable hope inside myself growing, growing, growing again. He kissed me at the door. Earlier he had sent flowers with a note that said, "Love you, Marc." I was prepared for a night that would make everything, all the horrors of the past, somehow vanish.

It was at about a quarter to ten that Marc began getting fidgety.

After a string of half-assed comments leading up to it, "I've got to leave," he finally said.

"But why?"

"Look, when I want to leave, I leave," he said. "Stop giving me the third degree. When I want to see you, I see you. When I don't, I won't. Tonight I just feel like going home and thinking some things out. You mean a lot to me, Rona."

He left. Two days later I heard that he'd gone straight to the house of one of my closest friends—one of my closest friends until I found out—and hadn't left until 4:00 in the morning.

But, after a period of partial healing, I tried one "last" time. Marc wanted to run for Congress. *This could be it,* I started saying to myself. *He's finally going to begin making himself into what he can be!*

I gave in, helped him in every way I could to prepare for it. But what he still required was the one thing he'd never had, that final symbol of American stability.

A wife.

"So what can I *do?*" he asked his backers.

The answer came back loud and clear: He could get a wife-to-be. Marc could become engaged. He would be running for a seat where a large majority of his constituents were Jewish. "And out here, especially because you're an obvious wasp," they told him, "the *ideal* girl would be Jewish. And the ideal Jewish girl would be Rona Barrett."

It fit like a glove. His two main backers came and asked me if I'd do it. I felt more torn than ever. Become engaged to Marc merely to further his career? What would be the real meaning of it to *him?* And to *me?*

I thought it rather ironic that the request was made to me while I was attending the wedding of Troy Donahue to Suzanne Pleshette. I was dancing with one of Marc's backers.

I decided to do it. If I could only give him that extra boost in his work, it might straighten him out as a man.

I went to bed that night, thinking of the next day when, after five years, I'd be engaged to Marc!

The following morning I rose at the usual time, walked

out to the courtyard to get the paper. I was drinking my orange juice when the page three headline hit me.

CONGRESSIONAL CANDIDATE ENGAGED TO MODEL

I wanted to die.

She was a beauty queen all right. Where he found her I wasn't quite sure. But his getting engaged to a member of Mannikins, Inc., assured me once and for all that I really wasn't Marc's type—I was too short, too unattractive despite Louise Long, too everything to become the wife of the future senator from the state of California.

I kept up my work somehow, but also kept on coming home right after work and throwing myself sobbing onto my bed until I fell asleep. Finally, Bob Marcucci convinced me to go to a party at his house. It would be the first time I'd gone out socially in five weeks. I'd taken almost no calls—particularly the ones from Marc. No doubt he thought he'd found some way to try and mend this most grotesque of his burned bridges. He had lost his judgeship and that's when the calls had really begun to come in.

While taking the short step to the entrance of Bob's house, my leg went out as if it were made of jelly. I sprawled into one of the shrubs, pain shooting through my ankle.

It felt like it was broken. It was.

Marcucci carried me into the kitchen. One of his guests was a doctor. He looked me over and made arrangements to take me to the hospital. While we were waiting, Marc walked in!

I could hear his voice from the kitchen. And I could hear the voices of two other girls who sounded like hookers.

Suddenly, he was in the kitchen. "Damn it, Rona, why haven't you answered my calls?" he greeted, not even noticing my leg and the physician.

"Leave me alone, Marc. I've just broken my ankle."

"Damn it, every time I need you, you're never there. Every time I've ever needed you, you desert me."

"Leave me alone!"

He pulled me out of the chair. The pain shot through my ankle again while he crushed me against his chest. He put his mouth against my right ear. "Just give me five more years and I'll make everything all right," he whispered.

I began crying. "I can't wait five more years, Marc," I sobbed.

For the first time, I made a "permanent" break with Marc. Even then, it took one final slap across the face— across both sides. Because, as always with him, I turned the other cheek. It came twenty days after Bob Marcucci's party. I guess my not wanting to wait five years had piqued him. So he moved in with a girl. Marc had done a lot of things, but he'd never *lived* with another girl while he'd been going with me.

I didn't see him for five years after that.

"Mr. Washington" was as different from Marc as a mountain from a valley. "Mr. W." *had* accomplished. He was a man of mind-boggling power and position, one of President Johnson's closest friends and cohorts. Within one meeting, though, I was confronted with a totally different relationship. Mr. Washington asked me to become his mistress.

I cannot begin to tell you how shocked I was by his immediate advances. It seemed as if I had always been on the other side of the fence, with a pencil poised, scribbling notes, listening to actresses relate stories like this. I never dreamed, though I dreamed a lot, that a man like Mr. W. would finally come into my life and say the things to me, little Rona Barrett, that he was saying.

He seemed so sincere.

I wanted to believe him.

I was so impressed just to be sitting in the same room with him.

But to become the mistress of a married man? No way.

And what audacity he had to even ask!

Here I was, a member of the press, maybe not a very important one yet, but certainly a member of the fourth estate, and capable of blowing a whistle on him that could resound back to Washington. But he didn't seem to give a damn.

The more I said no, the more determined he was to get me to say yes. But I held on to my pride and principles. They were the only things I felt that truly belonged to me.

No matter how unrealistic and self-destructive I'd been from Eddie Fisher through Marc, one thing I had learned from other girls' experiences: In the end a married man will punish his lover for her constancy! Why? Simple. Guilt. The more faithful his mistress is, the more threatened and guilty he feels about his wife and family. I'd seen it hundreds of times and with some of Hollywood's biggest stars.

I was boggled by him right off the bat. He not only had power, he had brain power. He rolled off vital statistics about American history and Presidents in particular as if he were the big Rand computer.

At first glance, he wasn't the best-looking man I'd seen

come down the U.S. turnpike. Yet he had this fantastic charisma, this way of looking at you that said, "It doesn't matter what I look like at first glance—I'm dynamite," that turned me on even more than if he'd been handsome like Marc.

By the end of our luncheon, I knew he was someone special. He called me that night from his hotel. He wanted me to meet him in Washington in two days, he said. He'd already called an airline and made reservations for me under an assumed name.

I told him no again.

Two days later there was a long-distance call. From Argentina.

"You're the only woman I could ever feel that sexual explosion with that I've wanted all my life, Rona," he somehow whispered and shouted at the same time. "The *only* one . . ."

Australia.

Bangkok.

Costa Rica.

The calls came every day. The tone of his voice became more and more passionate. Believable. I began fantasizing at long last my prayer was being answered. The big, powerful, wonderful, rich man I'd always sought, the man with the big brain and the big dreams, was going to sweep little Rona Burstein off her unsteady feet and carry her off to a never-never-land where no one was crippled, no one was unhappy, no one ever dies.

Except that he was *married*.

I asked him about his wife. His answer was as good as any movie speech I'd ever heard. "I waited such a long time to marry," he said. "If only I'd waited a little longer. How foolish I was to listen to my friends and marry for career and image. God, Rona, why do we always learn these things too late!"

I went to a friend for advice, an older woman. She said, "Why are you so damn proud, kid? What the hell has it ever gotten you except a few lumps in your gut? Listen, sweetheart, he's a big man. A big, big man. He's charming, and he's crazy about you. What have you got to lose? He's the kind of guy who can help. He can even *put* you at the top. Look how many years you've spent trying to get there. Where's it gotten you? Just older and a lot more cynical and not a dime in the bank. You say he's offered to help you get Hedda Hopper's syndicated column. Take him *up* on it. You're not a virgin anymore, sweetheart."

I took her advice.

A week later, Mr. Washington was in my apartment in Los Angeles making mad love to me.

At first, it seemed *heaven* with him, trite as that might sound. Unlike Marc, he was a consistent lover as well as a dynamic one. And how could he fail to help my career? But as the months wore on, it was obvious to me that I was repeating some kind of pattern, that beneath it all this man was exactly like Marc who was exactly like Eddie Fisher who was exactly like my parents who were exactly like—some part of myself, I guess. For even talking about him now gives me cause to wonder how much of that old feeling is still inside me. Not just feeling for *him,* but feeling that any association with a star, or someone world-famous, would have something special and good attached to it for me.

I'd never for one hour tried to use my body to get to the top. But in a way, I think my mind had been screwed long ago by those who had gotten there themselves—no matter what they'd done to make it—and so time and again I'd been led into rotten relationships and stayed the hell in them because of it. Oh, I very much wanted to *be* with the person. But, even more, I wanted to be where the person was in life. With Mr. Washington, as with the others, it actually ended up knocking me off my pedestal, rather than putting me on one.

With him, I was given that desperately needed feeling of reflected self-importance more than with anyone I'd known in the past, more than on the arms of the biggest stars in Hollywood at a premiere, or sitting in the bedrooms of the most famous women in the world hearing their troubles, or being invited to private dinners with the heads of America's largest corporations so I could "nicely" be given a crucial item they wanted leaked.

And I had needed him. To be what I *thought* he was.

Still, if he helped me in my career—

Well, dear reader, it turned out to be a personal disaster and an absolute zero for my career.

I learned, bit by painful bit, that he had a woman in every port.

Australia.

Bangkok.

Costa Rica.

Not only was there no thought of his divorcing his wife to marry me, but it turned out that when I cut away all the window dressing and the explosive orgasms and prestige, I was Mr. Washington's California Fuck-of-the Month.

He was shocked and angry when I broke it off.

But in the two years that followed, I made it to the top on my own. Much to his surprise.

But he repaid me.

Several years later, I was told by a prominent attorney that Mr. W. sat in on a meeting one day with every top executive in the motion picture industry and agreed that my voice should be stifled, that I was a bad influence on Hollywood and its community. He tried to destroy me.

The strange thing is, as I sit here now writing about it, part of me still adores him. No, he wasn't a god. He turned out simply to be a human being with strengths and weaknesses like any other *human* being. But bigger ones.

It wasn't easy climbing up the ladder without the partner I had always longed for. I hadn't had a real vacation in nine years. Christmas of 1969 I treated myself to ten days in Acapulco, having left ten generic shows in the can for syndication. Maybe my luck would change. Maybe my secret partner was hiding under a taco stand south of the border.

In the opening of the book, I told you what I was feeling in Acapulco. The last part of that scene was this: The following day I went down to the pool. Of all the people in the world who could have been there, of all the places on God's earth he could have been . . .

I was lying on my back in the early morning sun. I recognized him from one look at his muscled back. *Oh, my god, I don't believe it. I don't believe it! Of all places. Can't I ever escape him?*

As if I knew that someone's eyes were upon me, I lifted up and almost without blinking, said, "Marc."

He came over, bent down and kissed me as if nothing, absolutely nothing, had happened.

I felt married to Marc.

He asked me for dinner that night. I said "No!" I was

hostile. "How does it feel having four women in the same hotel who are all in love with you?" I asked. "You must feel very powerful, Marc." A former lover from a year ago was on the floor above him. She heard from a third party that he'd be there and had flown in. His newest mistress was in his own room, of course. A girl he'd met while staying at the hotel was leaving messages in his box every hour. As always, he was living dangerously and for the time being, the women loved him for it. The girl he was staying with, in fact, was not only married, but married to a man who was very thick with Aristotle Onassis and could really hurt Marc in business.

"Enough of that shit, R.B.," he said. "Dinner or not?"

"I'll see you around, Marc," I said somehow and walked away from him.

I left Acapulco immediately—I mean *at once*—so I wouldn't have to confront him again. I came home to California, shut off my phones and actually hibernated in my bedroom for the remainder of my vacation. On January 1, my private number rang. I'd only gotten it two weeks ago and had told *no one.*

"Hello, R.B."

"How did you get this number?"

"Happy New Year!"

I was silent for a moment. "Happy New Year."

"What about a drink for old times sake?"

I hesitated again. "All right. For old times sake."

We ended up at my house for dinner. He ended up telling me that his life had changed, that he wanted things to be different, that he realized once and for all how much he loved me, that I was the only person who had ever meant anything to him.

It was all true.

The problem with Marc was that he could only keep it true for an hour.

An hour was better than nothing. The man I loved was back. We hadn't seen each other for five years and during that period I'd made it to a peak, higher than I had hoped for. He loved me before in his own sick way, he loved me now. Who else ever could? The Marcs of life are something we can only do once.
only do once.

Like life itself.

He hadn't changed. I saw that the next night. We went to see a movie, then argued bitterly about it. It had to do with man's secret sexual desires. He hated it.

"Why do you hate it so much?" I kept asking. "That fellow played out every fantasy you ever wanted to do with me in bed. Isn't that *true?*"

The more I got into it, into him, the more defensive he became. It was *just* like the old days. The bad old days.

My love affair with Marc would always be the same. Like the girl with the curl in the middle of her forehead. When it was bad it was horrid.

But when it was good, it was a lot better than very, very good. In those few, rare moments—especially the sexual ones—it was *perfect*.

So I went back and stayed back.

For good.

Even though he hadn't changed one single iota.

What I didn't realize as I threw myself into him for that final time was that *I had changed*.

CHAPTER FOURTEEN

Though I began to recognize the familiar complex pattern of my life, it did not make things any easier. I thought, like so many others, that my problem was unique. That it was only happening to me. I could not believe that God had dealt me such an ugly hand at love. No matter who came into my life it all turned out to be shit. Mr. W. proved to be a deafening blow that took me a long time to get over. I only made things worse by going back with Marc. And on top of that, I finally found myself involved in the first lawsuit I ever had. The names of the people involved mean very little. They were really not in show business and while there was no maliciousness on my part in reporting the colorful life this gentleman allegedly led, I was painted by his prominent attorney and dozens of others as a horrible human being who absolutely had no business being a reporter or on television.

For two years I lived a nightmare. There wasn't a day that went by that I didn't spend half my time on the phone with lawyers or a lawyer wasn't standing in my doorway asking me another question and hoping I'd give him another answer. Through a loophole in New York law, the other side managed to attach my salary. There was only one thing they wanted more than the millions they asked for. They wanted me ... off TV. They even tried to make a deal with John Kluge, Metromedia's board chairman, that if he would drop me, they would stop the suit. Kluge, like Goldenson, told them where to go. He also told me—maybe forced me would be a more accurate way of putting it—to settle the lawsuit and get it out of everyone's hair. It made no difference to him or anyone else that I had not been proven guilty. That all the things the other side had accused me of were not true. Furthermore, Metromedia refused to acknowledge the fact that no one in their legal department had informed me that when I became a corporation I was no longer covered by the company's errors and omissions policy. Suddenly legal fees were now costing me more money than I had . . . more money than I ever dreamed of having in my bank account. In the end, the pressure became so unbearable and mingled with the hurts I had been experiencing over the years, I settled the suit. I just didn't have it in me to fight anymore. It cost me thousands and thousands of dollars. Dollars I worked hard to make. Dollars I didn't have. In the end I was forced to go to the bank for a personal loan. Metromedia had agreed at first to take the money out of my syndication, but finally decided against it. They refused to accept any part of the lawsuit as their own obligation except for around $7,500 which Al Krivin, the president of the TV division, gave me toward my defense and for which I will always be grateful. Metromedia Corporation refused to accept responsibility for the fact that it was their attorneys who approved my copy that fateful night, as well as every day prior or since, and knowing what they did about the story still permitted me to carry it. On some technicality, they, too, were not liable.

Those two years, as I've said, became a nightmare. Daily, I began to cut myself off from the stream of Holly-

wood happenings. I was too tired and too hurt myself
to care about the hurts of Hollywood. During the day
I carried on my business as usual, getting the stories I
had to, and despite all my aggravations, managed to have
better material than my competitors. How I did it I still
don't know. I guess if I hadn't built a strong foundation,
I wouldn't have made it. At night, however, I closed my
door to the town's nightlights. I didn't want to see anyone.
I didn't want to face the Hollywood I was no longer loving.

Most evenings I whiled away crying; other nights I
turned to mystics and the occult for temporary relief. I
probably interviewed more psychics and astrologers during
this period than I ever dreamed existed. There were only
four people I allowed to see me. Bob Marcucci, who had
now become my manager; Dorothy Brady, my then closest
friend who had become an expert astrologer; a former
literary agent named Alice Koehler, whom I called my
"udder mudder," and Marc. My other close friend, Shelly
Davis, had been spending much of his time in New York
getting his new production company off the ground. We
only spoke on the phone.

I had never taken pills. But for months I hadn't been
able to sleep. I had bronchitis, too, and it had become
really aggravated by my not going to bed as my doctor
had ordered. "It only takes a few minutes to tape my
show and they need it for syndication," I told him. "If
I don't do it, I'll screw up everything. I can't afford to
screw up." Every morning at 6:30 I would literally cough
myself up off the bed to begin my regular schedule. I was
getting such dark circles under my eyes that no amount
of makeup would cover them up. I couldn't even get
through a broadcast without breaking into hacking
coughs. Yet I was afraid that if I skipped even one day,

if I was off TV for just one day, everyone would forget me.

It was a Saturday, and Marc was to go with me to a fund-raising party for Share, one of Hollywood's oldest charities. After eleven years, he was going to do that. Or at least, he'd said, "Why not? I guess we could do that."

I had to go to Giorgio's in Beverly Hills that morning to get a jacket fixed. Marc was calling when I returned.

"You're not *going?*" I said, half in shock.

"No. Find someone else," he said. "I've got to go now." Then he hung up.

I'd never been so filled with hate in my life. All the hate that I ever felt for *anybody* or *anything;* it was as if it were all put together and then magnified a hundred times.

After Marc hung up, I had another coughing spell. This one wouldn't stop. I felt totally alone. I could not go to that—or any other party—alone again. Ever. Somehow I couldn't hear my own coughing after a while, could only hear people saying, "Why doesn't Rona Barrett have a boyfriend? Why hasn't Rona ever married?" I was sick to death of "escorts," didn't want my friends to have to take me to another party ever again.

I wanted someone of my own. All . . . my . . . own.

I looked at the pills. I poured out a handful. "The hell with it," I said out loud. "I'm going to sleep the weekend away."

I had stopped coughing momentarily. It started again. I couldn't straighten up. I felt myself shrinking, floating, frightened.

At that precise moment the telephone rang. I couldn't reach it. I fell against the night table, grabbed for the receiver.

I had it.

It was my best friend, Dorothy.

"Dorothy . . ." I said. "I am . . . dy . . . ing. . . ."

She found me in a semicomatose state.

She called an ambulance.

It couldn't find my house!

Finally, when it did, the driver sent out the message on the medical intercom system that they were bringing in Rona Barrett. DOA!

Dorothy said, "Damnit, she's not dead. I read her astrological chart, and she's not to die yet. *She's not dead.*"

I awakened four days later in intensive care—glucose tubes in my arm. My doctor, thank God, never left my medical charts out of his possession. So the story never got out.

However, my physician knew me well enough to inform one person: Marc. When the doctor reached him, there was a girl giggling in the background. "I don't believe it," Marc said.

"Well, you'd better believe it," my doctor answered.

Marc came to the hospital. Every day.

I didn't know why he did. When my doctor questioned him about our relationship, it was told to me much later that Marc snippily answered:

"Listen! Stop making such a big deal out of this. . . . After *all,* she *is* alive. . . . She's *not* dead, you know!"

"Yes, she's alive," my doctor answered. "But what kind of man are you?"

"Listen, Doctor, if you really want to know the truth Rona is one 1/1000 percent of my life. I'm a busy man. I speak to Rome and Paris and Lichtenstein every day of my life. I handle millions of dollars. . . ."

When I got home from the hospital, my dog, a Rhodesian Ridgeback named Lord, did not leave my side. Literally. For forty hours. He did not eat, he did not move his bowels or urinate. Seldom did he move.

In January of 1973 I stopped seeing Marc.

I did it without a letter, without a scene, without ceremony. I did it briefly, telling him, when he finally called, I didn't want to see him again. I did it without much emotion, partly because he had just about drained me of all the emotion I had. What remained was the instinct to survive—though that had been badly battered, too—and one small cell somewhere inside me which said, *This is the right thing, Rona. Even though you know tomorrow that you'll feel you'll die without him, if you just do the right thing, somehow it'll come out right. Someday.*

Marc began to put up one of his half-serious, half-flip arguments, but I cut him short and he stayed cut. He either knew I meant it this time, or figured that I'd be back as always.

I haven't seen him since.

CHAPTER FIFTEEN

It was October 8, 1972.
I was thirty-six years old.

Everything I had ever wanted to achieve for myself as a working individual I had virtually accomplished. After twenty-three years of total dedication to making myself a someone, a somebody, a person with position, respect, with the capability of earning real money, having what I said affect the whole country, it all seemed as if it were for nothing. I could hear my mother's words ringing in my ears: "So what good is all this when you come home to four empty walls?"

Over the years I had interviewed too many actresses, as well as women in other fields who had reached peaks, only to say to me: "Rona, I'm so lonely." Unless you've lived loneliness, you can't feel and understand its despair. It is like a black veil that floats above you. As one might picture the devil trying to peek through God's pure love cape. It floats above . . . looking . . . waiting . . . watching. And it never seems to fail to happen at the most glorious moments. At the most unsuspecting hours, it slowly drifts down and engulfs you. You are caught. Hopelessly caught.

After the pattern has repeated itself thousands of times over the years, the only consolation is that you know it has arrived. At least you aren't waiting for it anymore. And, when you are at a point of high understanding, you know in a matter of minutes, hours, days at the worst, that it will go just like it came.

Yet when it's there . . . the veil over you . . . oh, God . . . hell on earth aren't the words for it.

No matter how many times I tried to think of all the good things that had happened to me, I was totally incapable of doing so during the depressions. I just couldn't overcome the bad feeling. I hated myself and everything around me at those moments.

My thirty-sixth birthday was the worst I could remember.

When the alarm went off as usual at 5:45 A.M., I just let it ring. And ring. Until it ran down to a slower, weak ring . . . ring . . . ring. . . .

I was exhausted. I had spent most of the night crying. I was so unhappy that all I wanted to do was die. I didn't give a damn about the broadcast . . . about my parents . . . anything.

All I could think of were the eleven miserable years I had spent loving someone who had never really loved me. Needed me for a sick reason, yes. But loved me for *me?* No! I hated him, hated him more viciously than I had hated anyone in my whole life. How could one man be so evil? How could he have inflicted so much pain on not only me but the hundreds of other girls who had come into his life and been kicked out during the period he was with me. But the worst, by far the worst thing, was: *Why had I allowed him to do it to me?*

Lord, my beautiful dog, lay at the foot of my bed. I lifted myself off the pillow, swung my feet to the floor. My nightgown was drenched with tears and sweat and I wondered if the tears would ever stop. Lord sat erect. I looked over at him, whispering, "I love you, sweet Lordie.

Don't worry. Momma's gonna be O.K." He furrowed his forehead as if he understood every word I was saying, but was questioning their validity. "Don't worry, my big son. . . ."

And I walked to the shower with Lord following behind. I turned the water on. It was set for hot. I stepped inside, leaned against the cool tiles.

"Say Happy Birthday, Rona. . . ." I whispered to myself. "No one else will." And I slipped to the floor, cuddling myself against the corner of the shower, the stinging hot water pouring from the faucet at the same pace as my tears.

I don't know how long I sat there crying. But the water began getting cold. I reached up toward the soap bar and, as I had done so many times over thirty-six years, tried to lift myself off the floor. I looked like a small version of Lord.

But . . . I . . . *was* . . . *up!* I was *standing*.

And I was no longer crying. I couldn't even feel the cold water beating against my body.

I turned the faucet off. And stepped out of the shower. I reached for the towel.

Before I'd taken the pills, the depressions had been descending upon me with crushing regularity. They had become automatic the instant I walked into my home at night. Sometimes I would go straight through the front entrance, past my dignified Chinese couple, into my bedroom, locking the door behind me, turn on the TV so they couldn't hear anything, then break into uncontrollable sobbing for hours on end. No magic revelation came to me as I slipped into unconsciousness each time. No new-found appreciation of the value of life poured into me when I came out of it.

I loved life. I'd loved it since my first wracking pain at not being able to have what other kids had from life.

No matter what I'd done, that primal pain had returned again and again and again throughout my years, piercing deeper into me each time, depressing me more, leaving me closer to being helpless when only hours before—sometimes minutes!—I had known yet a new high, a really *greater* happiness from my achievements. The gap between my career and my personal life was finally too great to bridge. Having everything in my work made it intolerable to have almost nothing as a woman.

What would change that? Getting my picture on the cover of *Time* magazine? Moving into a $900,000 house?

I had never taken help in my life.

Ever since I could remember I had done everything on my own. *That* is what *my* life was all about, if it meant a damned thing at all.

Me.

Alone.

Pulling myself up by my own bootstraps every single goddamned time.

I had had a mother who wanted to help me with everything every hour of the day. I'd thrown off her brace, her doctors, her name, her home, her city, her.

In Hollywood, I threw off orgiastic temptation—a dozen times a day, some days.

I threw off my face, my body.

I threw off Marc.

And with *that,* I threw off part of Rona. A very sick part. Yet what remained, though I bitterly hated to admit it, was not independent enough, strong enough to survive.

I needed help.

The one thing I vowed never to do was to see a psychiatrist.

Going to a psychiatrist would contradict everything I stood for, destroy my innermost image of myself. Psychiatrists were for *weak* people.

Psychiatrists were one of the very few subjects, if not the only one, where I wasn't empathic. When a star mentioned to me that he or she was going, I'd shoot back: "They just fuck you up worse," or "Why would you want to do *that?*"

I was *afraid* to go to get help. I was afraid when *they* went for help, because it brought out my own need in bold relief—a need I couldn't face.

Yet I knew you didn't cast a short-order cook as the lead in a ten-million-dollar picture. Finally, I sensed that I needed *professional* help for my unhappiness.

When I went to see a psychiatrist in November, 1972, I didn't see that the *healthy,* the *strong* individual, is the one who asks for help when he needs it. Whether he's got an abscess on his knee or in his soul. I only knew I had better break my final rule—or be broken.

Sessions with psychiatrists are privileged information, not unlike priests' confessionals. But with Dr. G's permission, I taped one of our last ones. It's fitting that I should have done that, I think, because in a way everything I'd ever said or done was partly "for the record." For this book and what it represents to me.

I went to this analyst three times a week, two hours at a time, for six months. At the end of that period, I knew I'd never try suicide again.

Here is one example of why:

R: I've given a lot of thought to what we've talked about the last few times. What I think I see is that I would ignore negative "information" about a man I liked. Until it became so heavy and so obvious to me that I'd say to myself, "Why didn't I listen to myself in the first place?" Now I'm following my instincts a lot more. I figured it this way. If I was able to make such good value judgments about the people I was interviewing, if I was able to size them up so quickly and use the information which I gathered in a matter of minutes to find an even deeper truth, then why couldn't I do it with people who came into my life for other reasons than just to be interviewed!

DR. G: You also say that you have worked with a certain segment of society so long that you know them backward and forward. But in personal relationships, you hardly applied that at all. You wiped them out, didn't listen to them. As you didn't trust me, Rona. It sounds like it involves trusting *yourself* first.

R: True. Now, knowing all that, I guess what I'm really trying to say is that this is the first testing period I've ever had since Marc and my man from Washington. At the moment the thing I sense in the men I have chosen is their ability for *non*commitment, impersonal relationships. I was recently introduced to another extremely attractive man. He was presented to me as very influential, a great date for me—whatever they thought *that* would mean. But the person who introduced me to him knew me pretty well. I *thought*. I went out with this man. In one evening, I had such an intimate conversation with him that my blood boiled, my hair curled, and my toes twirled underneath. I couldn't wait for the evening to be over. It wasn't that I didn't want the intimacy, G. Oh, *how* I wanted it. But I just *knew* I had been spending four and a half hours with another Marc! When he asked me out again, I absolutely refused to go. I knew he would try to use me. I just smelled it. I recognized every sign, every symbol, though he was even smoother, I'll admit.

I was 100 per cent correct. The following day, on a vibe, I called down to Beverly Hills police. He had a record!

DR. G: Are you saying, Rona, that where you have felt most comfortable—where you're really with it when it comes to the human scene—has mainly been a kind of a cruddy structure with cruddy humans? The devious. The liar. The cheater. The stealer. The *impersonator*. Maybe that's the structure you know *too* well. Maybe until Marc or Mr. Washington were past, you hadn't enough opportunity to gain skill and ability in evaluating the structure of other kinds of people.

R: I think that's very right. I think my life has been filled with too many cruddy people.

DR. G: People's masks are invisible, but you are trying to lift them off, aren't you?

R: Yes. The only "crud" that I'm willing to accept is the knowledge that a man's Number One love is his work. If I'm Number Two behind that, I can accept it. I *want* it....

You know we started to talk the other day about fantasizing, dreaming and waking up feeling startled. Everything I ever wanted in life, I first dreamed. And then I got it. I would make it such a reality in my dream that when it finally happened in actuality—I mean, when I *made* it happen—it was always a great shock to me because 90 per cent of the time it was like *déjà vu,* very scary, extremely spooky. You know, when you're younger and you have no knowledge of precognition, when suddenly you're faced with a situation or walk into a scene and you know you've been there before, and you hear those words over and over again exactly like they were in a dream, it's very frightening!

Dr. G: I'm sure the unknown is always frightening. And you're telling me about an extremely powerful thing.

R: Yeah, the ability to make something happen for yourself.

Dr. G: Exactly. Just by dreaming it.

R: With Marc, I would dream seeing him destroyed.

Dr. G: You stopped being the instrument to keep people *from* looking at him as he really was.

R: Yes, but then I turned it around and allowed them to see him. It was like I was the master of his fate.

Dr. G: The power of destruction.

R: And that's the most frightening power of all. Because I don't like to see it that way, G. That's why it disturbs me when people have always asked me, "How does it feel to be powerful?" I never thought in terms like that. I guess it was just too frightening to think of it that way.

Dr. G: Look at it this way, Rona: As you were being what you thought was powerfully constructive for Marc by protecting him and concealing him, you were being simultaneously destructive to the people Marc dealt with. And to yourself.

R: Mainly to myself.

Dr. G: You breached your own rules. You did something for him you wouldn't do for yourself! And since you did it *for* him, you did it *to* yourself. You breached your own standards and your own ethics. *That's* hurting yourself. Rona, in a way you've been just as sneaky and as devious and as cruddy as all the people you deal with— but to *yourself.*

R: Does that make it any better or any worse?

Dr. G: It's the same thing. It's obscene simply because it's done to a human being.

R: But maybe it didn't seem so bad because I wasn't hurting others.

Dr. G: *You* know all about hurt, *you* could stand hurt, *you* could tolerate it. Right? Wasn't it great to know that you're doing it to yourself rather than having kids poking sticks at you?

R: That's true. That's what I really felt. I think it became very important to me to protect everybody from hurt.

Dr. G: No helplessness there. Right? By God, "*I* hurt myself, *I* do it to myself."

R: That's true. I was omnipotent, I felt that *I* had to determine who hurt and who did not. I think even in my work when I took out after people, I was the one deciding when they were bad, *I* was the judge and jury of their souls whenever they did something that did not appeal to me. But then that changed, too. That really, really changed. The interesting thing is that so many people still remember that old Rona. Those people, to this day, refuse to see the new Rona. Yet why is it that I still have this overwhelming desire to really set things right for mankind?

Dr. G: I think you'll answer that as we move down the road. Though making things right for the world would certainly mean taking the hurt out of it, wouldn't it?

R: Yes, definitely. But then again, if what we were saying before is true, there's got to be some hurt.

Dr. G: To appreciate joy?

R: I just don't understand ten-year wars like the Viet Nam situation, or eight-year wars like the Korean situation, or five-year wars like World War II. I don't understand why man has to inflict that kind of pain upon man in order to prove that there's a little joy out there. It *is* totally *obscene.* I mean we suffer enough hurt in our day-to-day relationships in just living. Why must we then heap it?

Dr. G: I think if Shakespeare were alive today, he'd still be writing the same kind of plays, trying to show people *themselves.* That was the way *he* did it. He tried to make things right in the world, too. It didn't work because one thing he didn't understand is that people are not really looking at themselves. They're going to enjoy the fact that it's "up there" and not "in here." The same reason kids watch monster movies.

R: But why are people enjoying Archie Bunker?

Dr. G: It's "out there."

R: All right, they want to be able to say, "It's not me, it's him." Like I'm the chameleon. I'm always escaping into a fantasy world when I'm not dealing hard with hard reality. And I always dream of it in terms of love.

Dr. G: You said your dreams changed in your early teens. They were always about someone loving you. Tell me about one.

R: It was like in the beginning when I developed my crush on Eddie Fisher. Then I went to work for him at thirteen, and I worked for him for months before I ever met him. He was not then the big star that he later became, but he was on his way. And at night when I would go to bed, I would see his face in my pillow or on the ceiling and I would begin to dream about what our first meeting would be like. I would dream and picture what he would do to me and what he would say to me and all I was concerned about was that he'd think I was really pretty. And that I would appeal to him and that he'd kiss me and kiss me and that I would wind up being the girl in his life.

Dr. G: He wouldn't see the monster in you?

R: No.

Dr. G: In a way, didn't you avoid ever being loved by someone who wanted to love you?

R: That was obviously the fault with Marc. I mean why was it that one year he desired me sexually and for two years he didn't? Why did he come and why did he go? Why did he tease me? Why did he taunt me? *Why?*

Dr. G: Did he see the monster?

R: I don't know.

Dr. G: That's what kids do with monsters. They tease them, they taunt them.

R: I don't know, G. All I know is what he did to me was extremely cruel. But I also felt that I was incapable of doing anything about it until I . . . just did. Helpless till then.

Dr. G: Maybe the real cruelty which you could not tolerate was that when someone like Eddie Fisher saw the monster helpless, he'd turn away in disgust. That would be the ultimate cruelty to you. Compared to that, taunting and teasing would be a paradise!

R: But why only with my lovers? Why don't my friends feel that way?

Dr. G: Do you fall for them? It sounds like *they* fall for *you.*

R: You're right. You're absolutely right. I must honestly admit that I don't think I really care for any of my friends the way they care for me. The last couple of days I've been having very heavy dreams about Mr. Washington. I get angry with myself over them. I actually feel his presence and his arms around me and his kissing me and sometimes he says, "Honestly, it's O.K. It really is O.K. I really do love you." It's like he senses that I'm

terribly apprehensive about his feelings and without my
having to tell him he says, "Honey, it's really O.K. Don't
worry about it. I'll take care of you." I had those same
dreams with Marc.

DR. G: I wonder if anyone ever did that with you
knowing the monster in you.

R: Yes, they did it, G. My mother and my father. In
fact the problem was *they* did it too much. You couldn't
experience anything without them picking you up and
saying, "Don't worry, don't worry." Little crippled monster.

DR. G: You've got a good memory.

R: Yeah, I've got a very good memory.

That was twenty minutes of what helped me to help
myself. Yes, it's disjointed. Like life too often is disjointed
because of the parts inside our heads that we haven't fit
together. But the most important help I gave myself *was
when I decided to go to the analyst*.

What you have just read, by the way, is a portion of
one of my last visits to my psychiatrist. As a matter of
fact, I told him that day that I felt I had gained what
I wanted and would only be back to wind up loose ends.
Not that he still couldn't give me more—but it wouldn't
quite be worth it any more.

"The pressures on me right now are too great," I said.
"I'm also feeling a financial squeeze. While I make a great
deal of money, my cash flow isn't what you think it is,
and shelling out practically $1,000 a month to you is
squeezing me to death and making me suffer so badly
that I'm finding myself with a whole new set of pressures
I never had before. It's just driving me bats, and obviously
that's the *last* thing therapy should do for me!"

"Don't let the money worry you, Rona. You can pay me any time you want," he answered.

"Unfortunately, since you above all know me, G," I answered, "you know that I can't do that. I cannot take your time and not pay for it now. We both realize that the future is a risk. Therefore, it's just not going to work. I feel that what I want to know, I know. You've helped me immeasurably to put the pieces of the puzzle all back together again. But I also feel that if I continued—above and beyond the money—I'd be wasting your time. To be frank, I just don't have the desire to see you any more."

"O.K.," he said.

There was one more thing. Brilliant and expert as he was, there was an edge now and then of his not being 100 per cent objective with me because of who I was. It was subtle, it was infrequent, but it was there.

They are human beings, not gods. The best of them would be the first to admit it.

But, oh, how I wanted a man who did not care at all "who" I was.

Only *what.*

CHAPTER SIXTEEN

I met that man one month later.

His name was Bill.

Bill.

What can I say about *him?*

Except that he was different from every man I'd ever met. A whole new thing. I'd been dazzled before, always disappointed.

Though very successful, Bill did not want what the world-movers and world-charmers wanted.

Yet he was more real for it. I think he chose it that way.

He was one thing more than anyone I'd ever met . . . *himself.*

And he made me feel, for the first time, like . . . *myself.*

What more can I say than that? It's because Bill is worth many more than a few chapters—more than a book, I hope—that I must make this chapter on him short. Because Bill has given me things that even I will not expose to the world. Everything in my life, from love affairs to psychotherapy to, yes, even close friendships, I ultimately threw myself into because deep down I sensed that I would one day be throwing it out to the world, in some way climbing another step toward the pinnacle through it. It wasn't planned, just an instinct.

That isn't true with Bill.

Bill is for *me,* not for *you,* tough reader.

We are very different in many ways. That's fine, just fine. Because friends can accept differences. And we *are,* above all, friends.

He's crazy about me, quite frankly. Sometimes I think he'd be crazy about me even if I were a telephone operator.

But should I marry him?

"Not tonight, Bill," I said. "I just want to be alone, got to get my head together."

I was a three-time loser.

Marc.

Mr. Washington.

And in a way, most of all, my father.

None of them had believed in me enough, none of them had been willing to see me for what I was. Each one went as far as he could in his own way—and it was damn far at times—but there was no breakthrough. And so they could not break through me.

Bill *seemed* different. *So* different.

But *was* he?

I can't stand to be hurt again.

But if not now, when? And with whom? There sure as hell would never be another Bill.

But what about Bill? What about hurting him?

I was like someone with an incurable illness where real love is concerned. My astrologer said so more than fifteen years ago. That was when I wasn't even twenty. Now I was thirty-six years old.

Thirty-six years old.

I walked through the rooms of my house, thinking. The living room. Perfect in its decor and neatness. I never went in it except when I was entertaining.

The kitchen. More to my liking. Bare wood showing, a hole where a fixture should have been—because I was remodeling it as I had five houses before it. It was my hobby. Much more important than the occasional look I would get from an acquaintance or star who exclaimed: "An unfinished room in Rona Barrett's house!" Because the stars I wrote about so often pretended, did that mean I had to pretend too?

The kitchen reflected my life.

It was ugly in spots.

But it was in the process of changing, and I thought it had a basic strength and honesty. Soon, I hoped, it would look really good.

The terrace with the swimming pool. It had a simple elegance and I liked it. But I was no longer impressed with it. Just as I was no longer impressed with Kirk Douglas' house on one side of me and Rosalind Russell's on the other. I *was* impressed with Kirk's enormous energy and intelligence. I *was* impressed with the valiant fight Roz was putting up against the horrors of rheumatoid arthritis. But those were *their* lives.

The library. Where I worked. Where I liked to sit with a few close friends I value. *This room looks like me,* I thought. *Bill is this room.*

I walked down the long hall to my bedroom. Oh, this room was me, too. But a me of sorrow. Could I ever make it into a room of joy?

I went back to the familiar safety of my library, closed my eyes, tried to form a picture in my mind—of Bill and myself.

But it wouldn't come to me.

I tried harder.

I took all the pieces, concentrated as I never had, tried to fit them together, one to the other to the other to the other . . .

They wouldn't fit. I couldn't make the picture.

That's when I saw it.

I couldn't make a picture of a *real* relationship!

That was the whole point.

I'd have to risk the final risk. I'd have to jump in head first, with only *some* of the pieces, and then *see* how things came out. Everything else in my life I'd been able to manipulate. When something had gone wrong with the picture, I'd wiped it out and "filmed" an even better one in my head.

That was why I had risen to the top in writing about *other* people's lives. And that was why I'd stayed at the very bottom in living my own.

I decided to marry Bill.

It was this book which got in the way.

It was this book—and everything it meant in my life— which catalyzed the first real fear I had about us.

The details are unimportant. What *was* important was that, as always, I felt everything seemed to be so right that it just had to go wrong.

Oh, *God*.

We stood in my library, at opposite ends.

There was only silence. Not merely the absence of sound, but something tangible, something that I had to break through and yet couldn't.

In desperation, I turned on the stereo, but almost by instinct pulled out an album Paul Simon had cut in England after breaking with Art Garfunkel and completing many years of psychoanalysis. I think Paul's problem lay in the album's first song, "I Am A Rock." My problem was the same. Essential isolation. Yet Paul had fallen in love. There *was* a girl on the album cover with him.

I put on the record.

The song ended. I shut off the stereo without pushing

the reject button. The beginning notes of the next song died with a low, disturbing drone.

Bill walked over to me, put his two hands just below my shoulders, pulled me to him almost effortlessly. He tilted my head up so that I was looking into his eyes. "I don't buy that item, Rona. In fact, I'm not really interested in the Rona who editorializes—through a record or a movie or whatever it is. I want the real Rona."

I wanted, more than anything else throughout my life, to find the truth. In this book, I desperately hope I've done it. I have written literally millions of words for almost twenty-five years. Here, on these pages, I tried to open myself up as much as a human being possibly can.

The first time I ever did that in my life was with Bill in that moment.

There were no guarantees that I wouldn't close to him the next morning, the next hour, the next moment. But I didn't close *then*. He wasn't asking for a guarantee. He was asking for *me*. I have no eloquent, original, beautiful phrases to express what I felt in that moment. I said none to him. All I can say now is that for the first time in my life *all* of me felt like a woman. Loved. By a real man. All I could do was stand on tiptoe and whisper in his ear, "Oh God, Bill, I'll try. I *want* to be that Rona. I want a man who wants me to be *that* Rona."

He took my hand and we walked out of the library, down the long hall to the bedroom where so many times I had lain and sobbed, where once I had lain dying from pills.

For the first time in my life, one part way way way inside of me didn't feel alone. Has Rona the Rock begun to crumble?

*Talk to me of love, Bill. I've never heard the word before.
I'll cry for you, Bill. But don't make me cry too much.*

I had left my library, my books, my poetry, Rona Barrett. Just as once I'd left Rona Burstein. I was naked. Unprotected.

Bill closed the bedroom door behind us. The bedroom where I used to hide.

My pain had vanished. I forgot every tear.

Will you protect me, Bill? I am a woman.

I sat down on the floor!

I couldn't get up by myself, not without looking like a paralyzed dog. I didn't care. I would let this man see me that way. Or even help me.

He sat on the carpeting next to me. He tickled me. I laughed.

In the winter of 1974, I bumped into a business associate of Marc's. A *former* business associate, I should say. He exited his particular deal with Marc about eight months ago. He told me everybody else was doing the same, that Marc was tremendously in debt without a real prospect in sight.

Because Marc's prospects were really always people, and now his reputation was preceding him wherever he went. Oh, he could still be good for a one-night stand—or even a one-month stand—with some chick who didn't know the score.

Marc will be forty-five years old this fall.

EPILOGUE

Bill and I were married on September 22, 1973, in Beverly Hills. I became Mrs. William Allan Trowbridge.

I'm writing these final words in my library late on a Thursday night. Bill is in Reno on business. Tomorrow I will fly up to be with him.

My physical condition is the same today as when I was born. I've only learned how to do things better. Once I decided not to remain a "mental cripple," my handicap didn't appear so blatant. I developed back muscles which enable me to lift my legs as if I were almost normal. I still can't walk steps like normal people, nor can I run or jump or skip rope. But an adult doesn't have to do those things. That was my compensation. And thank God for the automobile—its use covers a multitude of scenes and sins. Secretly, however, I still die whenever I'm forced to walk a flight of stairs in front of other people. I've even turned down guest appearances on TV shows where I would have had to climb a podium. I never told anyone the truth about that—until now.

I just watched myself on TV. The thrill never lessens.

But my capacity for thrills has grown. I need greater achievements. I desperately hope that in some way this book will be the beginning of that. By telling even more of myself than I ever told of the stars, by telling *everything,* in one way I have burned every bridge from the first thirty-six years of my life.

Yes, it scares me. More than a little. It's a risk, tough reader.

But not quite as great a risk as trying to kill yourself. My marriage is a risk too.

Bill has turned out to be everything he seemed. More. But I'm still a manic-depressive.

I am still someone who, no matter how high I climb, always sees a higher pinnacle.

And that part of me, I guess, no human being can reach.

I say that with regret.

I say it with exaltation.

What I'm telling you, tough reader, is that I can't wrap it all up in a Christmas package with tinsel and a ribbon. Some days it *does* have a Hollywood ending. Other days, it sure as hell does not. *Those* days, I often sit here with Lord, and feel as alone as I'm certain any person feels.

Lord's eight years old now. Once he was a magnificent show dog, had a number of blue ribbons, simply a magnificent creature. Now he's a garbage disposal, just a big old fat garbage disposal.

Right, Lord? Right, Lordie?

You love me don't you? You love me, my big little boy.

I hope you never die, Lordie. But I know you will.

I cup his head in my hands. He's as gentle as cotton. To me. He's bitten about a dozen people, from stars to deliverymen, even bitten a couple of friends he'd gotten to know well. I think all of a sudden he just didn't want to take a chance on them hurting me.

Right, Lordie? You love me, don't you, my son?

The phone rings.

I pick it up. It's a fellow writer from the Midwest who's become an intimate friend rather quickly.

"How are you, Rona?" he asks with great meaning.

"You know how my life is," I answer.